Retail Arbitrage:

How to Make Money Online with Proven and Powerful Strategies in Today's Market! Create Passive Income with Amazon FBA, Affiliate Marketing, eBay and E-Commerce!

Table of Contents

Introduction

When more and more people are threatened by poverty and live paycheck to paycheck, something has to change radically in order to get out of this messy situation. It's really hard to imagine people without debt nowadays, as almost every adult has at least one credit card. Living in debt is something that we are getting used to, but do we actually like just "surviving" from one paycheck to the next?

There are plenty of people looking for extra income, something that can easily support or provide the lifestyle that they want. The internet is packed with opportunities, but we are not always choosing the right ones for us. Our life choices define us and help us pick the right or the wrong path in life. It's amazing how many people honestly believe they can get rich overnight by investing in some kind of multi-level marketing (MLM) scheme or some kind of fancy Ponzi scheme. In most cases, these get-rich-quick schemes are total scams, so you need to stay away from them and not to invest any money or time in them.

If you want to become rich, you cannot achieve this by gambling or playing the lottery. If you do want to become an entrepreneur, keep in mind that a business is all about taking calculated risks, so you are not gambling with your money for investment;

you are using your money to generate more income in a lot safer and secure way compared to gambling.

Some of the popular ways to get more money online include vlogging, social media, crowdfunding, but the most solid way is to sell products online. You can find plenty of ways to monetize your website, but if you do want to make real money, then selling online is what you need.

Trading has always been the most profitable activity on the planet. That's why merchants are the wealthiest people in every city. Some of the greatest companies nowadays are retailers, and this can only let you know how powerful this business is. Therefore, selling products online can be the best way to get rich and to become a successful entrepreneur. The idea is very simple: get a product from a source (supplier or manufacturer) and sell it to end-users at a higher price, and therefore mark your profit. Repeat this activity over and over again. Sell more products, earn more money, and have a higher profit. The sky is the limit when it comes to selling online, especially with modern-day conditions. Whether we like it or not, we are currently experiencing a shopping frenzy when people tend to buy a lot, even though they don't need the products that much. We have become addicted to shopping, as we tend to spend more money than we can earn.

A huge chunk of sales is done through credit. People are now using their credit cards or personal loans to buy more stuff. Some of the purchases may be determined by an urgent need, while others may be encouraged by a ridiculously low price. Trading seems to be booming now more than ever. That's why sales are through the roof on both physical and online stores. Opening a store, physical or online store, seems to be the most inspired decision when it comes to business, as you can take advantage of the shopping fever that most people are experiencing.

I don't know who set the trend, but we tend to spend money that we don't have to buy things that we don't really need in order to impress people we don't care about (most of the time). Apparently, this is how everything started, and the main reason why trading businesses are booming. This is also why technology is encouraged to flourish and evolve. We are hungry for more and thirsty for the latest released products, even though we may not know how to use them. Always wanting new products and getting the best features seem to be the ideology of consumerism. This is what drives today's trading, and it seems that this moves things forward.

If you do choose to open an online store, you choose to be a very small player in a huge game. However, nothing stays forever, including your status as a small merchant on this market full of opportunities. You can adapt to the latest changes and grow, or you can remain behind until you find yourself off the market. This book is all about giving you the right tips to maximize the potential of online sales and how to get more money using the tools available out there.

From sourcing your product that you want to sell to selling it on different sales channels, this book includes all the information you need to stay in the game and be a better player. It emphasizes on the solutions provided by Amazon (FBA) and provides tips on how to use your webshop and try other sales channels. This book should be your bible for online sales.

Chapter 1: Choosing between Retail Stores and Buying Online

We do have to admit that we shop now more than ever, and more and more people are becoming shopaholics. There are so many of us who tend to spend more than they are actually earning. Most of us already have credit cards, and it seems like we abuse these payment instruments and use them to buy a lot of things. How many times have you heard someone buy a product just because it was on sale? That person might not have an immediate need to use the product, but they bought it because it was a great deal. You might have the same problem, as you probably shouldn't have bought that pair of shoes when you already have a few other shoes (in perfect condition) very similar to the ones you just bought.

Truth be told, the marketing departments of retailers (physical or online stores) have us hooked, and it looks like we are addicted to shopping. The modern-day conditions are all set up for consumerism, so the products we buy will not last very long because the parts they are made of don't have good quality. After intense use, the product will not function because there is at least a part over there that is not working.

To fix the issue, you might want to change the part. However, the cost of it is often very high, so you are more likely to buy a new product, and then you use a credit card if you don't have the money for a down payment.

Just think of a smartphone. If you damage your screen, then most likely the cost of the repair (including the new screen) will be too high for you to pay, so you think of buying a new product, probably from the same manufacturer. If you don't have enough space on your iPhone, you can buy space on iCloud, or you can upgrade your phone to a newer version, with more space on it. Either way, you will end up spending some more money.

When you buy a video game, you may choose just the basic version (sometimes you can purchase some sort of a bundle that includes extra features), but if you want to fully enjoy everything that the game has to offer, you will need to pay extra. Modern-day society is set on consumerism, and retail stores (physical ones) and online stores have the most to benefit from this shopping frenzy. Shopping has become a very complex activity. That's why you can find all kinds of stores grouped together, just to offer a better shopping experience for the customers. This is what the shopping centers or malls were designed for — so people can spend a lot of hours to shop but also have some fun while doing it.

Malls have become great places to hang out, socialize, buy the latest products, watch the latest movies, or even have a tasty burger. You have to be immune and to resist all of these temptations in order to go in there and not spend a single dime. Shopping malls have flourished throughout the world, but at least in the United States, there aren't too many of them being built at the moment, at least not like in other developing countries, where people are new to the "magic" of shopping malls.

When you are going to the mall, be prepared to spend some time over there, as you simply can't expect to get out of it after five minutes. Some people might say that the era of physical shops is about to end. I wouldn't say that, although online stores make tons of money and have plenty of customers. Spending time at the mall will still be one of the most preferred activities for American families. It's like an all-inclusive tour, as you can purchase some nice shoes, watch a movie, or even have a burger or pizza, all in one place.

Because time is precious, when you do want to shop, you want to do as many things as you can. Clearly, shopping mall managers don't have anything against this; otherwise, they wouldn't rent space to all kinds of shops, restaurants, or other vendors. Nothing beats proximity when it comes to shopping. So why walk or drive a lot to get from one store to another when you can find anything you need in one place?

Time means money, and in this case, spending more time in a shopping mall, most likely will lead to spending more money. There are times when you feel too lazy to go to the store and buy yourself a pair of jeans that you want or the shoes that you always wanted, or you simply don't have the time, as you are probably working two jobs to pay your bills, loans, and rent.

Luckily for you, there are plenty of options to buy online, so you don't even have to leave your room. All you need is a device connected to the internet and your card nearby. You are determined to buy and know exactly what you are looking for. Also, you know your size for shoes or clothes, and you trust that the retailer will not sell you clothes or shoes that don't fit you. You go on your favorite online store — whether it's Amazon, eBay and so on — and look for your favorite products in there. This is the way to shop nowadays, as everything you need can be purchased in a matter of minutes, and you can enjoy the rest of your time doing something productive, or just relaxing in the comfort of your home.

Since the use of mobile technology has evolved over the years, more and more sales are done from smartphones and tablets. You can be in your favorite coffee shop or in public transportation on your way to work. Every moment you are connected to the internet, it can be the perfect time to check the latest offers and perhaps even buy your favorite products. Just "add to cart" and wait for the courier to bring you the stuff you ordered. Most online retailers try to deliver within 48 hours. Some retailers even have a same-day delivery option. Sounds pretty nice, right? So why do you need to go to a shopping mall and spend plenty of hours over there to check for your favorite products when you already know what you are looking for and you can have the product you ordered the next day or possibly even in the same day?

Some people would think that online shopping takes the fun out of shopping, as you don't get to try the jeans, shirt, or shoes that you are buying, you don't get to feel them before you buy them — you only trust the merchant that he will send you the product matching the pictures, description, and size. True shopaholics are addicted to retail shopping, visiting shopping malls, and spend a lot of time there.

Occasional shoppers can live without going to the shopping mall and purchasing lots of products from these stores. As long as their credit score is good, shopaholics will always have credit cards to use on these purchases. Thanks to them, the brick-and-mortar retail stores are doing really good, and businesses are booming for some physical stores. You can find below some interesting statistics provided by the U.S. Department of Commerce Statistics (Ward, 2019):

- Total sales made by the physical stores increased from $3375 billion in 2016 to $3496 billion in 2017, having a 3.6% increase.

- There was an increase in e-commerce sales from $390 billion in 2016 to $453 billion in 2017, meaning a 2% increase.

Shopping preferences (physical stores or online shopping) can be different from one age group to another.

- Millennials prefer to shop online, as 67 percent of them would choose this method.

- 56 percent of the gen-Xers are more in favor of online shopping.

- Baby boomers are less interested in online shopping, as only 41 percent of them prefer this method.

- Just 28 percent of seniors prefer shopping online.

Although online shopping is very popular among young people, still most of the sales are done in physical sales, and the value of sales is growing each year. The physical retail market is split between many key players, and at the moment you can't say that there is a merchant that rules with absolute authority this market. Although there are a few with a larger piece of the market share, no one is that powerful to dominate the market. Therefore, the competition is fierce, but there is still enough place in the market for new companies. In the online world, things are a bit different. Amazon is the absolute leader of online retail, and there isn't a company that can dispute its supremacy online, at least not in the United States.

For many of the buyers in the United States, a purchase starts with a product search on Amazon. With approximately 100 million Prime members and a number of customers that are getting closer to 500 million, Amazon is a world leader in online sales, selling almost every possible product you can imagine. When you provide such diversity, it's clear that you are going for most of the market niches.

There are plenty of reasons why some people prefer to shop online, especially the young generation:

- It's 24/7 shopping. You can shop anytime, as long as you have an internet connection.

- It's a money saver. Online shopping allows you to check several offers at the same time and decide what store you can buy from.

- You don't have to worry about transportation to the mall and back or where to park at the mall, as online shopping doesn't require a physical presence.

- It's a time saver. Imagine how much time you would spend when going to the mall. You need to try on clothes or shoes, and you need to visit several stores until you can finally buy the product that you want. You don't have to worry about anything like that when buying online, as you can buy the bag, a pair of jeans or shoes that you want in a matter of minutes.

- It's convenient. There are so many people who dislike crowded places and don't feel very comfortable with undressing and trying on clothes in a store inside the mall. For all these people, the solution is very simple. They can buy online from the comfort of their home.

- When you don't find the product you need in the shop you visited, you might be tempted to try at a different shop. When you shop online, it's easy to see if a product is available or not, and if it's not, you can quickly find another online shop where it's available.

- For orders above a certain limit, free shipping applies for some online shops. Amazon has its Prime members for which shipping is free. Of course, they will have to pay a monthly subscription, but overall, it's totally worth it, especially when they are frequent buyers.

Most of the statistics above already indicate that the physical stores are doing really well these days. Sales are booming, and a lot of money is spent in these shops. But why are there plenty of people still preferring this way of shopping? You can find out these reasons below:

- It allows buyers to physically interact with the product before buying. They can try it, test it, feel it, and so on. This is how they can make a judgment call, and they don't have to rely on the opinion of others (reviews). When they are buying food, the recommended way is to buy directly in the store, as you can check if the produce is fresh or not or if the fruits you want to buy are recently picked.

- Products can be obtained immediately after the purchase, so you don't have to wait for them for 24 hours, 48 hours, or even more.

- You have the opportunity to ask a sales representative more information regarding the product, so you will be informed straight from the source before making any purchase.

- You don't have to worry about any shipping costs, as you will pick the product directly from the shop.

- You will avoid the unpleasant situation of getting a product that doesn't fit you or doesn't match the description or picture. So you will save yourself from all the hassle of returning a product.

- If you do have to return a product, the process is a lot less complicated compared to the online shops, as you can just come back with the product in the same shop (or another shop if it belongs to the same chain of shops and their policy approves it).

- You can't ignore the experience itself, as shopping in retail stores, like the ones from malls, can be a very fun activity, and you have plenty of other activities you can combine, like eating in a restaurant, drinking your favorite coffee, or watching a movie.

The current condition of today's society encourages most of the merchants to have an online presence, so if they have a physical store that is doing pretty well, why not have another sales channel online? Some of these merchants are more adapted to the current times than others, so not only do they have a very successful physical store, but they also have a fully functional online store (fully optimized, probably integrated with Shopify) and an account on Amazon and eBay to boost the sales and get the most out of both of these worlds (physical stores and online shops). On top of that, there are plenty of businesses that already have a social media presence (Facebook page or Instagram account).

To maximize the potential of each shop, it's essential to combine the physical stores with an online presence (webshop, Amazon/eBay marketplace presence, and Facebook/Instagram account). Therefore, if you are already familiar with the physical version of the store, then you are probably comfortable buying online from them because you already know what kind of merchandise they have. There are different opinions, just like there are different people. There are buyers who prefer the crowd. They want to socialize and interact with the sales reps and to get all the info regarding a product directly from the store. For them, shopping is all about getting more than a glimpse of the product; they want to try everything the product has to offer before purchasing it. Nothing beats the sensation of trying on clothes, to find out how they feel on you, and they are willing to dedicate a large portion of their time to experience this sensation before making the purchase itself.

Other people are not too keen on going to dressing rooms and trying seven shirts, jeans, or other clothing items. They don't feel too comfortable to undress and dress again inside a store, although they are doing this from a dressing room, behind a curtain. This is why they stick to online shopping, as this kind of shopping can be done in a very discreet way, without having to step out of your comfort zone and give away your intimacy.

Online shopping can be done from anywhere — from the comfort of your home, from your favorite coffee shop, or when you are going to work in public transportation (not while you are driving). You only need a mobile device or PC with an internet connection. Whether you want to choose physical shops over online shopping (or the other way around) really depends on the time you have available to spend, or on your beliefs. At the moment, both of these shopping methods have increasing popularity, but slowly, online shopping is becoming more and more used. You can imagine that senior people are not that used to technology, so they don't buy online. They probably don't use a credit card, just a debit card, to withdraw money from the ATM, not to use it for purchases. The good thing about online shopping is that it offers more options for payment, so this is a plus. However, there aren't too many people using e-wallet systems to make payment (by e-wallets I mean payment instruments like PayPal, Skrill, and so on).

Chapter 2: Buying Online — Key Facts to Get You All Set

The internet is the source for absolutely anything, including products you want to sell later on. There are so many methods to make money online nowadays, so it's really hard to choose from these methods. In the civilized world, almost anyone has access to the internet — to this never-ending source of information, products, or services. People are often too naive and fall so easily into temptation, especially when they are not informed properly. That's why there are so many going for all kinds of MLM schemes, which are not selling anything at all, just a crazy idea that I'm surprised is still catchy. Some of the most popular ways to make money online nowadays (and legit ones) are the following:

- Selling products or services online, which is the main topic of this book

- Monetizing your website through advertising (advertising from Google)

- Crowdfunding

- YouTube

- Instagram

- Facebook

In my opinion, the best way to make money online is to sell products or services online. You might not even need a proper space to conduct your business, like an official office, store, or warehouse, as you can do this from the comfort of your home, from your basement or garage. Sounds too good to be true? Well, trust me, it's true! The internet can offer endless opportunities. You only need to notice them. As people tend to spend more money and shopping, even the money they don't have, it's definitely the right time to get in this game and to profit from this shopping frenzy. You might be scared at the beginning, as you are new to this and you are entering unknown territory, but life is all about choices. It's only up to you if you want to live paycheck to paycheck or you want something else, like financial stability and freedom. You are taking a risk, but this risk can totally pay off, and you might find yourself making more money than you ever imagined.

Everything has to start with an idea, so think about it! What product(s) would sell like hotcakes? What business would make you feel like you just hit the jackpot? It's all about noticing demand and request. Perhaps it can just hit you one day. "Hey, I really need a product like this, but it's not available anywhere." Perhaps you are just dissatisfied with the product or service you use, and you are convinced that you can do better than this. It may sound strange to you, but this is the starting point of every business, especially one like an online store.

So you've already made up your mind. You know that you want to sell online, and you also have a very clear idea of what you want to sell. What's the next step? You will need to create a start-up company specialized in online retail and register your company with the authorities so that you have everything all set from a legal and tax point of view. Be extra careful when you choose the name of your website or your business. The name will have to be very catchy but also project professionalism, so be very serious about it.

Now that you have these details taken care of, you will need to look for professional web hosting and web development services. There are so many solutions to hand. Some companies prefer the use of platforms like Shopify (which can also get you a domain), Magento, and PrestaShop to create the online store that they are dreaming of, while some of them want something purely original without having to use a special template so they hire some developers and pay for web hosting. Nevertheless, you have taken care of your legal tasks and now you have your very own website to get you running.

The real fun part is when you are looking for the products you want to sell. First, you will need to find manufacturers or suppliers to provide you the products you need to sell on your website or on other sales channels. You really don't need that much to buy products online or the spare parts that can lead to the products you want to sell. Online purchasing requires a computer, an internet connection, and a payment instrument. Every search starts with Google, as this is the most popular and most used search engine on the planet. You don't have to bother yourself to understand how Google works and how it displays results (at least not at this point). You have to type in the search query what you are looking for. It's better to search for products with high profit margin. You don't want to sell online chewing gum, which has a very little profit margin. This is why you need to do proper research on the products you want to sell before you set things in motion. But at this point, let's focus on the necessary steps of buying online.

Step 1: Search a product on Google. Type in the search query of Google the name of the item you want to buy and then click "Search." The results will display a whole range of websites — from the most famous ones to the least known ones. You might notice that famous websites come first. This is because Google takes into consideration the traffic of the website first when displaying the rankings.

Everyone can search for widely used products. You are probably searching for the same products also, but you are not interested in buying one product — you want to buy in bulk to get a price per unit that is a lot better than the one on these famous websites.

That's right! Just because these websites are popular doesn't mean they provide the best price. There are plenty of cases where they simply offer a price higher than other websites.

Of course, Google will take into consideration your location, so it will offer results from your country. But who says you are limited to your country? If you are reading this and you are from the European Union, it's better to purchase from another country of the European Union. Why? Because you will not have to pay extra taxes, so you don't have to worry about customs or other additional taxes (if you are properly registered).

The language barrier can be an issue in this case, but you can find interesting products in other countries that are cheaper than your country of residence, for which you don't have to pay customs and VAT (a form of tax in the European Union). This is why you need to search on the Google page of other countries as well. Get the most interesting offers, and put them all together into a comparison tool. The price will not be the same because each company has its very own profit margin to think about. They might have the product from the same source, but the prices are different. However, you are not looking for the product, in particular — you are looking for a company that can supply you the product in bulk (so at a considerable amount).

You are not going on Amazon and put 50 identical products in your shopping cart. This will cost you a lot more compared to when you are buying from suppliers. On these shops, you will need to pay on the spot to receive the order. With suppliers, they can issue you an invoice, for which you have a due date to pay it. When your company is new, suppliers may not be that patient with you to pay for the order, so they want it paid as soon as possible. However, as soon as your company has some years of activity, suppliers will leave you the merchandise, and you can pay it later — perhaps they can wait for you for 30 days.

Products in the United States may not be that cheap compared to other markets, but luckily for US companies, they can source products from suppliers or manufacturers in Mexico — thanks to NAFTA. Labor costs are a lot lower in Mexico, compared to the United States or Canada. That's why you can still see plenty of products in the United States that are made in Mexico.

There are plenty of American companies working with Mexican companies and getting products or services from them. The Chinese market is also quite tempting, as you can find over there manufacturers and suppliers, but you have to worry about overseas shipping, custom taxes, and so on. Sourcing products in China is still a very profitable activity, and there are plenty of American companies, especially big corporations, that are depending on imports from China. It's really up to you how and where you want to source your products, but truth be told — the internet can provide you endless opportunities, and you can use it to get in contact with all kinds of suppliers. If you want to sell clothes, then it's highly recommended to search for companies in Mexico that can manufacture the products you want. But this is just an example. When you do want to purchase high quantities of goods, you have to look for wholesale websites. This is why you will need to create an account with one (or more) of the following websites:

- 4WholesaleUSA

- BAOlink

- Greatrep.com

- Top Ten Wholesale

- Closeoutcentral

- ToyDirectory.com

- Wholesale Directory

- Wholesale Hub

- Alibaba.com

- Wholesalers4u.co.uk

Chapter 3: Using Technology and Graphs to Your Benefit

If you plan to sell online massively, you will have to be very active when it comes to acquisition, as you will have to purchase products massively from your supplier or manufacturer. Obviously, you will need to step in the current times and use technology for mostly everything — from accounting and stock management to procurement. Some of these solutions are all integrated into CRM or ERP systems, so anyone using this technology can appreciate the features provided by this kind of software. Automating supply processes seems to be the latest trend in plenty of companies throughout the world. These technologies are very useful for increasing productivity, cost efficiency, and visibility. When you have very complex operations, e-procurement software can help you improve the efficiency of business transactions and the negotiation leverage for companies.

The use of technology is one of the most powerful signals for company maturity. There are plenty of tools you can use for e-procurement. Most of them have similar features. Here are some key advantages to using e-procurement software:

1. Lower costs and better spend visibility. E-procurement software can better track products from suppliers and centralize this data in order to get a higher volume of items at a better cost for the buyer. This software can enable you to track cost reductions and find out any gaps and address them, all on a continuous basis. When we speak of this kind of software, there are some KPIs involved — meaning that it will show some key process indicators of your business. You can see the *track vendor SLAs* if the products and their prices are compliant with the contract. Scorecards can be implemented. All of these can lead to higher savings and enhanced productivity from suppliers.

2. Operational performance. E-procurement systems can lead to the automation of all internal procurement processes, like purchase order tracking and supplier evaluation, and this will definitely lead to higher operational efficiency. Imagine the time you save on these processes if they are automated — they won't require human intervention.

3. E-catalogues and increased standardization. Suppliers tend to promote their products using electronic catalogs with very accurate information about the products displayed over there. The use of catalogs leads to the standardization of products, as these catalogs are becoming more popular. E-procurement software will allow you to compare standardized products from different suppliers.

4. *Internal integration.* The purpose of using this software is to create better collaboration between departments, increasing the value to the organization. This kind of software rules out any kind of discrepancies, so data remains accurate for all of the departments involved.

5. *It helps a lot with documents.* E-procurement software stores the contracts, invoices, quotes, or other files related to product procurement so they can be used again for other orders, quotes, or contracts. Imagine how much time you are saving here when you don't have to start a document from scratch — you can just take an older document, edit it, put the right details, and *voila*, your contract/invoice (or other documents) is now ready!

6. *More accuracy for your data.* When these processes are done automatically, you eliminate the human error, so there are a lot lower chances of getting errors in the documents generated by these systems. As long as the details are accurately introduced, you don't have to worry about such errors — unless your software provides some kind of errors that are not related to human use. When your system as a repository of documents, you can check previous orders or contracts to make sure they comply with the terms and conditions of your contract and, therefore, eliminate all inaccuracies.

7. *Global procurement.* Imagine that you have to source for products in different countries, so you have to deal with different languages and currencies and different options for logistics services. This is an extremely difficult job, and if you don't do it properly, you can generate some serious errors. So why cheap out and try to do this task manually? Why not use an e-procurement system for all of these tasks? Proper e-procurement systems can support different languages, logistics options, and languages, so why complicate yourself with doing these procurement activities in a different manner?

8. Standardized workflows. The e-procurement system can implement a workflow (and standardize it also) in order to minimize any deviation from the process. There are some benefits of using this software, like making sure that all of the transactions are done through the right channel or making the approval process a lot easier. Also, such a system can track existent suppliers, check existing contracts, and prevent any purchases that can be done off-contract.

In order to implement this kind of software into your system, you will need a specialized company to sell you and integrate the software. Some of these companies may have their very own in-house solutions for this type of activity; others can only integrate already-famous software programs and customize them to your needs. Depending on the cost of these services, you can select the right option for you, but make sure you check the features also before deciding solely based on the price.

Chapter 4: Search for the Best Prices

When you have a retail store and you sell in your brick-and-mortar shops or online, your profit margin is directly influenced by your cost of acquisition. Nowadays, the main focus is all about maximizing profits. That's why many companies are in some sort of reorganizing process and departments are being reduced to cut down on costs. Plenty of people have lost their jobs for the sake of profits. It has always been like this, and frankly, as much as we hate to admit it, businesses are all about profits and not about employees.

However, now you've evolved from being an employee and living paycheck to paycheck to being someone who manages your own business. There are plenty of things you will need to consider, such as the volume of sales, cash flow, turnover, and profits. When you operate your business in retail, in order to have higher profits, you will need to minimize your costs of acquisition. Therefore, you will need to scan the market for the best prices out there in order to maximize your profit margins.

You simply don't want to know about supply and demand or how they can influence the prices that you are getting. When you buy products, you are also paying the manufacturing costs (cost of labor and utilities), the price of spare parts, and so on. When you buy straight from manufacturers, they can make you an offer that can cover all of these costs. You can imagine that these costs are not quite low in the United States. That's why merchants are trying to find products elsewhere. However, low prices should not be your only criteria when searching for products, as the quality of products should be even more important than a small price.

Of course, the ideal situation is to find good quality at very good prices. Now that's a great deal! But finding great deals is not an easy job. The beauty of sourcing products and product procurement is that there are so many suppliers and manufacturers, and there is an unbelievable fierce competition between them. Naturally, they are trying to get more customers, and the price factor seems to be the most decisive one in order to get more customers. These manufacturers can make you a good deal if you are looking to get more products at the best prices out there. Although it may seem a bit odd, you can still find great deals sourcing for products in the United States. There are plenty of wholesalers that can offer you amazing deals, so it all depends on the quantity of your purchase. The more you buy, the better price per unit you will get.

Obviously, when you are about to start your business, you can't buy an incredibly high number of products, as you don't know how well they will sell. You probably won't have enough storage space, or you probably need to rent more. Although it may sound very tempting, try not to fall into the trap of overbuying because you don't want to spend your whole budget on getting really cheap products. That money is better spent on marketing and advertising campaigns and on making your website extremely functional and appealing.

Remember, you buyers need to have the shopping fever, not you. You will have to be cautious when buying. Try not to spend too much of your budget on the acquisition. After all, that's why you are searching for the best prices. Don't just stick with one wholesaler — check the offers from all of the wholesalers you know. The more offers you get, the better.

Although price is very important, don't ignore the quality of the products. If some wholesalers have a proven reputation of providing poor-quality products, then you will need to rule them out. You need to filter offers first based on the quality of products in order to compile your very own shortlist of products. Once you have the shortlist, now you can take a closer look at the price per unit, compare the features, and decide which supplier or manufacturer you want to work with. You can work with more than one supplier or manufacturer; you don't have to stick with just one. In the years to come, if you sell a lot of their products, manufacturers and suppliers will offer you higher discounts or better prices when you purchase from them.

The profit margin is indeed offered by the difference between the retail price and the cost of acquisition (how much you pay per unit for getting the product from the supplier/manufacturer). But the true profit is made through the volume of sales. The more you sell, the higher your profits will be. Interesting fact! The more you sell, the less you will spend on the unit price per product. Suppliers or manufacturers will offer you a better price for a larger-quantity order. If you are not satisfied with the price of products, you can also source for products outside of the United States. Mexico seems to be a very interesting market. China is heaven for finding products. There are plenty of merchants who are using Alibaba.com to source for the product they need. When choosing your supplier or manufacturer, there are a few things you will need to consider:

- *Communication.* This is a very important aspect, especially when you are dealing with foreign suppliers or manufacturers because the service you receive also matters a lot. Good communication can increase your chances during the negotiation process, so you can have higher chances of getting a better deal.

- *Quality.* When you are searching for products, it's highly important to check the quality of the product, so you need to ask for some samples first to make sure that the product matches your requirements and has the quality you want. You are selling products through your own store, so your reputation is at risk at well. You need to be remembered as the merchant that sells "the good stuff." If you are constantly appreciated for your products, your customers will buy from you over and over again.

- ***Price.*** This doesn't have to be the decisive factor, so it would be a lot better if you negotiate on a good-quality product instead of settling for the cheaper product but with a lower quality. So don't cheap out and select the cheapest product. Go for the one with the best quality per price ratio.

Chapter 5: Maximize the Use of Social Media

We all know that Maslow's theory of needs has five layers: *physiological, safety, love or belonging needs, esteem,* and *self-actualization.* Recently, you can also add the need for being connected, as this seems to be the latest trend among all of these people. Social media is part of our lives as we replaced the standard way of socializing with virtual interaction. Truth be told, we can hardly imagine life without social media, as such websites are platforms where you have all-inclusive entertainment. So you won't see just profiles of people; they offer a lot more features than that. These features include instant messaging, live streaming, games, GIFs, advertising, marketplace, fundraising, events, offers, and so on. You can barely imagine a place that has all of these features included.

Let's face it! Social media is addictive, and we are already addicted to it. We check our profile several times per day from our smartphone, tablet, or PC. If everybody is on social media, so are the businesses. Social media enthusiasts would probably say that you don't exist if you don't have a social media profile. It's the same with any business. If you want your business to be promoted, you really have to abuse social media. Since all sorts of companies are promoted through Facebook or Instagram, you can also find business partners through social media.

Do you know the kind of website where you can just post ads and buy stuff? If you take a look on Facebook Marketplace, this is what you will find — plenty of ads of items on sale. You can even find stores and many other products that can be sold. As you probably already know, Facebook analyzes your behavior on this social media platform. It knows what you like and what you are looking for, so it can have several suggested or sponsored posts for you.

Again, this is based on your behavior online, as you have your list of liked pages. Nowadays, most news articles are read from social media, from platforms like Facebook, as the user has liked the pages of some online publications. If you like the pages of any business, you will most likely subscribe to their feeds, so you will receive the latest news and posts from them. Therefore, social media can be used as a huge source of information, especially for companies looking to buy products. Such companies can visit the Marketplace section of the platform, discover the latest posted ads, or search for different wholesalers on this platform. These suppliers or manufacturers have every interest to be present online, so they have a very attractive Facebook page, packed with all the latest information.

Most probably, such suppliers or manufacturers already have a fan base of persons or companies that liked their page on Facebook. Everybody in the fan base will receive the latest news, so the posts on this platform are considered just as notifications or newsletters sent to their customers or potential customers. However, this is just the tip of the iceberg, as Facebook is not just about liked pages and the marketplace. There is also a special section on Facebook that can include offers and promotions — everything from holiday offers to plastic surgery. Chances are, you can also find some interesting products on sale from wholesalers. You are probably aware of wholesalers that are selling all kinds of goods, not just food or drinks (these are probably the most common). You don't want to sell food or drinks online. You need to sell something that is a lot less perishable — something that lasts a lot more and doesn't require special conditions for storage.

So far, we've learned that social media can be used for advertising, posting, and receiving news (liked pages). It can provide valuable information that you can use for sourcing. But this doesn't even come close to Facebook's (or other social media platform) main functions, which are instant messaging and communication through comments. You can easily contact a supplier or manufacturer on Facebook through Messenger and find out everything you need to know about the products you want to buy.

As you already know, communication is vital when it comes to sourcing, so why correspond through emails when you can get all the information you need through Messenger? It can take days to finish a conversation through emails, so it's slower to get all the information or approvals you need. Emails should be used for a formal approach (to sound more professional), but to get things done, you can use a more direct approach — contact the supplier or manufacturer directly on Facebook and find all that you need in a conversation through social media.

Customer support service is a lot more effective through phone and live chat, as you can address all possible queries at one time. It goes the same with social media, so the exchange of replies and information are done in a much faster pace compared to sending emails. Business correspondence is the exchange of emails, which seems to be the most formal and official way to communicate between two companies. However, this can take forever, and you probably don't have the time for this. You probably need information in the fastest way possible, so you can pick up the phone and call the manufacturer and supplier, or you can chat with one of the representatives from the wholesaler or manufacturer.

A chat eliminates any misunderstandings, as written information leaves no space for interpretation. Having a chat on social media with the rep from a company is like having a face-to-face discussion with that person. You can discuss all the important matters over chat, get all the information you need, agree on terms and policies, and just exchange emails to confirm everything you've discussed and to send over contracts and invoices. This is why if you have the chance to discuss over social media with the supplier or manufacturer, don't hesitate. You can speed up the process and get things done a lot faster than using just emails.

You do understand that time means money, so why waste time on the endless exchange of emails when you can have an agreement after one discussion over social media (in the most fortunate cases)? However, most of the time, you will need to discuss a few times in order to have a deal. Social media is not just for entertainment; it's a lot more than that. It's a very powerful tool to get in touch with suppliers or manufacturers, discuss with them frankly, and speed up the process. Imagine that every day that you delay the launch of your products can be the help that your competitors need. So you don't want to waste too much time on the sourcing process — get things going as fast as you can.

Social media can be used for so many things, and it can also increase the efficiency of your business. You shouldn't rely just on social media to conduct your business — you need to create your very own mix of tools and techniques in order to increase productivity, efficiency, and organization of your business.

Chapter 6: Count on Google

Google has already become a synonym for *searching online*, as you "google" something on the internet. If you don't know information regarding a certain product, you *google* it. Can you imagine the internet without this search engine? I certainly wouldn't. Although there are plenty of other search engines, nothing comes even close to this one. Just like any search engine, Google displays the search results according to rankings, and it uses a special algorithm to filter the results and display them in the right order.

Most people have Google as the landing page when they open their browser, so for them, Google is the gateway to the internet. There are probably hundreds of millions of active websites out there. Most of them are filtered by this search engine. Since there are so many of these websites, Google will need to take into consideration some criteria in order to display products appropriately. There are too many websites that are more or less optimized, but traffic and location seem to be a few of the most solid factors that influence the rankings on Google.

You can imagine that Google will not display the first results from a different location. Also, you probably noticed that the websites with the most traffic are displayed first (Google studies the clicking habit of everyone and knows exactly which websites have the most traffic). This comes as no surprise to you, as you know that if you search for a product online, the first results will be from Amazon (if the product is sold by Amazon). But Google is not just optimization; it's a lot more than that. There are also ads posted on Google that uses the same principle as the pay-per-click (PPC) advertising. In other words, you can bid on some keywords to purchase a spot for ads on the first page of the results. Every click counts to your traffic, especially when you have an online store, as this is how you can increase the visibility of your products or brand.

Since most of the online searches start on Google, plenty of companies have decided to place ads on this search engine because it's the place where you can find everything. Unless data is protected by some kind of encryption and trademarks, Google can easily display the data you searched for. When you are a merchant trying to find products you want to sell online or in your physical store, Google will give you a hand. With the right keywords, you can find plenty of information you need, including suppliers or manufacturers. Google will find their websites, or if don't have any, it will find their contact details. But don't stick to your local version of Google, as this search engine can be found in any country. Keep in mind that you will find first the results from your own country, but if you want to source for products abroad, then you might need to search for a different location.

Google has plenty of tools and extensions you can use, mostly with their very own browser, Google Chrome. This browser allows you to use all kinds of extensions, and some of them are very useful for your sourcing activity. You can try DROPSEEK and OAGenius, incredible tools that you can use for sourcing products. It's really no wonder that Google is one of the most powerful companies out there, as anyone has heard of it and everyone is using at least an app, extension, browser, or tool from this company. This search engine should be step 1 of your sourcing process, as the internet can provide you endless opportunities and information, and Google is the path to take advantage of these opportunities and to access this information.

Google comes in every possible language you can imagine, but if you want to search for products in a different location, you might need to change the domain from ".com" to something else. You can try the Mexican Google if you want, as Mexico can still be a very interesting market for sourcing products, especially because of the cheap enough labor force. Merchants can search for suppliers and manufacturers in countries known for their cheap labor force. Mexico is the closest country to the United States that has lower paid labor force for the manufacturing part, but it may not be cheap enough. That's why people search for products in the Asian market.

China is the most popular market where you can find all kinds of suppliers and manufacturers. Of course, you may not be familiar with the Chinese language and alphabet, but you don't necessarily have to switch to the Chinese Google in order to find the suppliers and manufacturers you need. Keywords can make a difference in this case, so you can still type in English and get results of such companies from China. You don't have to switch to Google.cn to get these results. If you type in your search query the kind of product you are looking for, as well as the manufacturer or supplier, and then finish with "China," the search engine will know exactly what to display for you, so you will not see results from the United States. As a general rule of Google, the results will be displayed in the language of the search query, so you can even type in English on Google.cn and still get sufficient results in English related to your query. Google can also be used to find out the biggest trends at the moment in terms of products and brands. It can help you understand the search volume and the interest for so many different products.

Chapter 7: Use Amazon for Sourcing

Don't get your hopes up, as Amazon is not the place where you can buy products in bulk. Amazon is a platform dedicated to end-users, so you are not buying a whole pallet of the product you want to sell. This is a marketplace dedicated to selling products, so don't buy products on Amazon for you to sell on the same platform. However, there is still a way for you to use this platform for sourcing products. You are probably asking, How is this even possible?

Amazon is not considered the best place for you to buy products for selling, but it can provide you plenty of ideas for choosing the right product that you want to sell on this platform. There is no better place to get the inspiration you need when choosing the products you want to sell online. This marketplace can provide you a lot of interesting information, as you can conduct market research procedures on the products you were thinking of selling. You can use the existent tools you have on Amazon to get all the possible information you need.

In order to be successful, you will need to find a successful product and also take into consideration the supply and demand. Therefore, if this product has a high demand, how many merchants are already selling this product? What is the volume of sales for this product? Do you see a few merchants or possibly just one domination the market? You need to understand what you will be up against before you even start selling on this platform. Gather as much information as you can (you can find it through the use of tools) and use this information to perform your very own SWOT analysis. There is no better time to perform this task, as this is how you can come up with an objective conclusion about your chances of selling on this platform and still making a handsome profit.

When you decide on the kind of product you want to sell, you will need to find first the best-selling categories on this marketplace and take a look through the products displayed over there. This is how you can find your inspiration, as you can see plenty of popular products and you can easily see how well the best-selling merchants are performing. When the product you are looking at is being sold in a higher quantity and there are already a few merchants with too many reviews and sales (you can confirm this information when you use the tools to find the volume of sales and a lot more information about your competition), you will need to forget about selling this product. Don't be naive and an incurable dreamer! You need to assess your chances properly, as you don't want to enter a market where there is already a key player calling all the shots. You can't prosper in this kind of niche market.

The type of market you should be looking for is the one where the top-seller doesn't have too many sales, so the market share is split differently (well, not quite evenly, but something close to that, where you feel you stand a chance). It will probably take you days to find the ideal product for you, or perhaps just a few hours. Either way, the product you are looking for should respect the following criteria:

- It should be a fast-selling product, as you need to think of storage costs. A slow-selling product will not be in your best interest.

- Size and weight matter. Try to find products that are not too heavy or too big. Not only will you not sell these products very fast, but you will also have difficulties when it comes to shipping these products. The carrier will charge you a lot to deliver these kinds of products to your customers, not to mention the storage space you will have to pay for.

- Try to stay away from season products. Seasonal products may sell like hotcakes during their season, but they can't sell the same when the season is over. You want sales all year round, not just for a few months, so these seasonal products are not for you — unless you are selling an additional inventory for which you want to get some extra cash.

- Price matters. Most specialists would agree that products between $25 and $50 are the best-selling ones on Amazon and on other sales channels. Don't try to tackle the niche of luxury products! You need to have a reputation and to be known by rich people (I'm talking about your brand) in order to be successful in this market niche. Try to make your product more affordable for most people because this is how you can increase your sales significantly.

- Try to avoid overcomplicated products like electronic devices, as there aren't too many manufacturers out there qualified enough to make the product that you want, plus these products will also need technical support. Are you qualified and specialized enough to provide this type of service to your customers? Probably not. At least in this case, the simpler your product is, the better, because your product will have to be functional and user-friendly.

- You may need to research this in-depth, but the ideal product is the one that can offer you a higher profit margin. You probably don't know exactly how much your product will cost when you buy it straight from your manufacturer and supplier. However, you can try to find some information related to this topic, which will help you to estimate your profit margin and serve you well in the sourcing process.

- Stay away from perishable products, as you probably can't sell them fast enough in order not to alter before being sold. Plus you need special storage conditions so the temperature inside the warehouse will have to be just like in a refrigerator or freezer.

Amazon will provide you the information you need in order to get the best products for you to sell on this platform. It may take a few hours or a few days, but after browsing through all kinds of products, it will suddenly strike you. You will get the idea of the product you want to source and then sell online. Any idea has to start from somewhere. You need to get inspiration from all the possible sources you can think of. I'm not saying to stick just with Amazon, but this platform probably has the largest selection of products a retailer can have. You can find a product in there and say to yourself, "Hey! I already know a few people who can benefit from this product! But there aren't too many choices on Amazon! What if I develop my own product and then sell it on Amazon?"

You can probably see an opportunity where other merchants don't. It can be a product that is not too present online, so you can come up with such a product and sell it to the people who need it. Or perhaps you notice a product that doesn't have the quality you would expect, and you say to yourself, "Hey! I can do better than this!" Most likely, your product will not be unique, so you need to make sure that your product is better than the available options on the market. You have to be convinced of this and also to convince your customers about this. Involuntarily, Amazon and its merchants can provide you plenty of ideas you can use for your products — not to mention that you can find suppliers or manufacturers using an SKU code or the exact title. This is how you can compare the product with the one already being sold on Amazon. The tools you can use will provide you information about the quantity sold, so you can make some calculations about the quantity you will need to order.

Chapter 8: Why You Should Still Consider Alibaba

When you are thinking of starting your very own online shop, there are only two things you need to have in mind — your product idea and your sourcing method. The previous method already explained how you can use Amazon to get the right ideas and how this product should be like in terms of price, size, weight, and many other aspects. Your product ideas will need to have market viability — that's why you need to spend hours and even days on Amazon to find the product that's right for you. Sourcing for products is definitely not an easy task, but luckily for you, there are four ways to do this task:

- Make

- Manufacture

- Dropship

- Wholesale

Alibaba is hands down the best place to source for products. It's the world's most famous B2B (business-to-business) marketplace. It's the ideal place where companies from all over the world can meet Chinese manufacturers and suppliers of all types and sizes. No matter what product you think of selling online, no matter the quantity you want to order, on Alibaba, you can find not one, not two, but plenty of manufacturers capable and willing to work with you and provide you the exact product you need in the right quantity. This platform is the most important playing field for businesses of all sizes and from all countries around the world.

China is the world's leading manufacturer, as most of the products made today are "made in China" or have at least one component that is made in China. Now, you are probably thinking, "Wait a minute! Chinese products have poor quality. Why would I want products from China?" Unfortunately, this myth was spread around the world for centuries — that Chinese products are all cheap and with poor quality. However, Chinese manufacturers are also very capable of making high-quality products. Want to bet your own iPhone has parts made in China? The myth of poor quality is about to be busted, as most of the companies sourcing for products in China are very satisfied with the quality they receive. You are dictating the quality of the product, and these Chinese companies can easily comply. The cost of labor is incredibly low in China. We are talking about a huge country with the largest population on earth. Just imagine how many people are already involved and work in production facilities throughout China. Even with extra tariffs on imports from China, sourcing products in this country is still totally worth it.

Let's say that you've already found a product you want to sell among the most popular ones and you are determined to sell it from now on. You've already validated your idea by asking yourself a few simple questions about the product (if you can sell it, if you can ship it, if it's not too big or overweight, or if it's not seasonal). You don't have to do this whole step by yourself — you can ask your family, friends, or other people you know. Find out who will be your target audience and how many products do you think you can sell in a given period! If the results are satisfying enough, then you will need to move on to the next phase — the sourcing phase.

There are three ways to source for products:

- Direct wholesale

- Privately branding

- Dropshipping

The sourcing process has to be very successful, and therefore, it has to respect some of the following criteria:

- It has to be easy.

- It has to ensure low costs of goods in order to get better profit margins.

- All products have to be reliable and have high quality, so they need to be tested.

- In order to grow with your business, the manufacturer has to be scalable.

If these are the sourcing criteria, then you need to set the requirements for the product (I may be repeating myself, but these requirements are very important for your business). The following are the product requirements you have after validating your idea:

- The product will need to be easy to ship and light.

- It will need to have lower costs in order to ensure a higher profit margin.

- The product doesn't need to have health risks, so forget about selling electronic products or food.

- It needs to have a demand and a market. Google Trends and the people you know already helped you with this.

- It must have a place where you can source the product.

Now you will probably ask yourself, "Great! Now what are my options for sourcing products?" If you prefer dropshipping, then you can choose Printify or Printful, you can try local wholesalers or manufacturers, or you can head to the greatest wholesale marketplace on the planet, Alibaba.

There are so many merchants who choose Alibaba for their product sourcing, and you can find below why:

- This is the perfect place to find plenty of reputable manufacturers for the product you need.

- Alibaba has a very strong reputation worldwide.

- This platform can provide you rules and regulations to make sure that you or your investment are safe. Alibaba filters manufacturers and suppliers from China, making them respect the regulations and rules set by this platform. You can rest assured that every manufacturer or supplier over there is legit. There are options for trade assurance, reviews of manufacturers, or different security levels — all of these make you gain more confidence in this platform.

- Low on budget? Don't worry! Alibaba can help you out, as most of these suppliers and manufacturers have very reasonable prices — plus you can even negotiate a lot of them.

In order to start sourcing for products on Alibaba, you will need to follow the next steps:

1. Register with Alibaba. In other words, set up your account with Alibaba. This platform doesn't have the language set to Chinese, so you can easily use the platform as it's in English. Registering with them is pretty easy and straightforward because you can easily set your own ID and password.

2. *Understand Alibaba.* You need to find out what this platform can offer and who you are dealing with here. There are two types of companies present in this marketplace. The first type is factories. It's the manufacturer that can make your goods for you. There are plenty of these factories that have their very own sales teams designated to deal with merchants like you. These are the kind of companies where you can get the best deals. The second type is trading companies or suppliers. This kind of company will head over to the factory, buy the products you need, and sell it back to you. Finding a factory to manufacture your goods can be a bit difficult in some situations, but trading companies can help you out. Perhaps, if trading companies have a special relationship with some factories (since they bought plenty of products from them), there is the possibility to get great deals from them because they can buy the products from the factories at special discounted prices.

When trying to find the right company to manufacture your products, you will need to select more than one company in order to compare the best offers. Most of the factories or trading companies present on Alibaba are very flexible and open to negotiations, so you are definitely in the right place to source for products.

3. Be smart when you source for products on Alibaba. Every decision you make when sourcing products here will impact the success of your business. There are a few steps when sourcing for products here:

- Finding a supplier

- Picking a supplier

- Contacting the supplier

- Ordering a sample

- Testing your sample

- Order a massive quantity

There are a few terms you will need to get used on Alibaba — it's highly recommended for you to know them, as they will help a lot in this process of sourcing products.

MOQ (minimum order quantity) requirement on this platform mentions the lowest quantity that a manufacturer or supplier is willing to sell to you. When MOQ is not met, then you need to rule out this manufacturer or supplier.

OEM (original equipment manufacturing) is when you provide the full specs of the product you want, your own requirements, and your visions related to this product. The manufacturer will use them to make your product from scratch. If you want a unique product to start your very own brand, this option is a must when you source for products.

ODM (original design manufacturing) is when the factory creates your product based on just a few ideas from you, so they are also making the design and don't have to follow any specific requirements. The factory will suggest the product, and if you like it, you can order it.

Trade assurance should cover you when you have a dispute with a supplier or manufacturer. If you submit your claim to Alibaba, they will take a look over it. If the factory didn't stick to their promises, they will refund you. The trade assurance is something that has to be set at the beginning of a sales agreement, and it has to include the points that you find to be crucial for your business (and that are worth disputing), like lead times, QC, and so on.

Gold supplier is when the factory paid Alibaba to become more visible in the search results. Alibaba has its own advertising process, and manufacturers and suppliers can take advantage of it, to have higher rankings in the search results.

Assessed supplier is a result of an evaluation done by a third-party company that visited the company to check out their equipment and facilities.

QC stands for *quality control*, and this is where Alibaba exaggerates as they take this process extremely serious. There are a few types of QC processes:

- **IQC** stands for *incoming quality control*, and it applies to raw materials or parts that enter the factory in order to be used in the manufacturing of products or goods.

- **OQC** (outgoing quality control) is applied to the finished goods that are already ready for shipment.

- **QC and QA** (quality control and quality assurance) represent how quality is controlled and assured during the whole process.

- **IPQC** stands for in-process quality control, and it's done during all phases of the manufacturing process.

FOB (*free on board* or *freight on board*) represents the cost of delivering your goods to the nearest port, but the buyer is responsible for shipping the product from that port to his address.

CIF stands for *cost insurance and freight* and means that the seller must pay for the cost of shipping, including insurance, to bring your goods to your port of destination. Once the goods are loaded on the ship, the risk is supported by the buyer.

Therefore, when you search for products on Alibaba, you need to select some of the options mentioned above (e.g., trade assurance and gold suppliers) and the minimum order. It's the perfect time to pick your supplier, so you will need to consider a few aspects, such as the following:

- Price

- Minimum order quantity

- Time listed on Alibaba

- Time listed as a gold supplier

- Reviews and reputation

Once you have viewed some factories or suppliers on Alibaba, it's time to check their website, just to make sure they are legitimate. Find out how detailed their webpage is and how it's structured. Check for pictures of the factory, detailed information about the location, or more information related to their history. Can you see any image of their products, any professional descriptions? Do they say anything about delivery times or the QC process? There are also fraudsters and scammers on Alibaba, but a thorough check will prevent you from dealing with such companies.

If you are satisfied with what you see (both on the marketplace and on their websites), it's time to contact the manufacturer and supplier. For this process, you will need to compile a list of the best companies you found on this platform that are related to your product search. When you reach out to these companies, you will need to follow some simple communication guidelines, such as the following:

- Keep it short and effective.

- Make sure that you introduce yourself and your business.

- Tell them what you are interested in (provide requirements, specifications, and ideas).

- Ask about the cost of samples and delivery times.

You can tell a lot about the company you are dealing with from the communication process. This can give a first impression about them — whether they are true professionals or amateurs. Sometimes, a friendly tone can make a difference when nothing else can. You can notice if they project confidence and trust when you inquire them about all the possible details you need. If they are hesitant, then stay away from them, as they are not professional or are amateurs.

Regardless of how you interact with them and how friendly they are with you, it's important to always ask for samples. You can't rely on trust, at least not at this phase. Ordering samples can be the first step of a long and mutually beneficial collaboration. If you are not very keen on paying for a sample and shipping it all the way to you, then perhaps you shouldn't be sourcing for products in China. Samples are important to your business, as they can set the product template you want, and you can have an option to see, feel, and test the product you want to order before buying a massive quantity of this product.

For shipping, many manufacturers or suppliers like to work with global names like FedEx, UPS, and DHL. If the sample is exactly the one you need, meets all your requirements, and has high quality, then it can be the first product from your order because your first order can make you pay for the whole lot, minus the sample. Manufacturers and suppliers often charge merchants for samples, as this can be an extra guarantee that the merchant is serious enough to have a collaboration.

At this phase, you don't trust the company you are dealing with, and the Chinese companies don't trust you as well. Mutual trust and respect can be built over time, as you order a lot of products. The more you order, the better prices you will get. The communication between both parties has to be very effective in order to speed up the process, so when you email a manufacturer or supplier with your queries, most of them reply within 24–48 hours. Based on their reply, you can check if they answer all your questions, if they communicate clearly enough, or if they meet your basic requirements. Your first contact most likely will be by email, but if they are responsive and interesting enough, you can switch to another means of communication, like Skype or

WeChat — something that can get you the answers you need a lot faster. At this point, you can use emails just to confirm orders, to exchange documents (e.g., contracts and invoices), or to keep it formal.

Communication can create a special bond between you and these Chinese companies, as it can start a beautiful collaboration. However, empty and sweet words making promises and not sticking to them will not build the collaboration you want. The sample plays the most important role in finding the supplier or manufacturer you want. This is how you can see whether these companies can stick to your requirements and follow your guidance. The sample is just a small challenge for these companies. In order to speed up the process, you will need to order samples from different companies, just to have something to compare. If you order just a sample from one company, there might be some chances that the sample doesn't meet your requirements.

Since you're ordering the sample from China, it will take a while for the sample to reach you, although it's being sent with fast couriers. However, to wait to receive one sample that isn't according to your requirements is just a waste of time. You will need to order samples from five to ten different companies and then compare the samples. Sure, you will spend some money for the delivery of all these products, but you seriously increase your chances of getting the product you want. You will need to see the samples, feel them, and test them in order to select one supplier or manufacturer.

Some Chinese companies are very professional, and they will reach out to you to get feedback from you. The sample will rule out any scammers and fraudsters, so if you mean business, you will definitely embrace this step, as you will know for sure who are dealing with. It goes the same for these Chinese companies because the sampling process will let them know that you are very interested in collaborating with them. It eliminates the non-legitimate customers for them, plus they can get new customers while the shipping costs are supported by the buyer. Payments on this platform can be done by credit or using AliPay. Trade assurance can guarantee that you will not be charged until you receive the goods.

If you are satisfied with the sample, you will need to contact the supplier or manufacturer that sent you the sample and start negotiating. These companies are usually open to negotiations, so you better keep this in mind when you have to choose a product that is within your budget but has a lower quality or when you have to negotiate the price of another one with higher quality but with a higher price that is outside of your budget.

Still, before you ask for the sample, you will need to choose between ODM and OEM, as you want to sell these products with your own label. If you just want to stick your label to an existing product, this option is called ODM (original design manufacturing). If you want to design a product from scratch, this process is called OEM (original equipment manufacturing).

The sample will let you know how well these companies made the ODM or OEM product. When you have more samples to choose from, it's a bit harder to choose the right one, as you are faced with a tough decision. You might like them all because the quality is about the same for all these products and their prices are similar. Hence, you need a tie-breaker — something to increase the odds of choosing a product and not another one. You will need to negotiate will all these companies to get the best deal. At this point, you negotiate the price per unit according to the quantity you are ordering. Also, you will need to consider the issue of shipping. As this massive order can only be sent by sea, it will take some time to reach you. The manufacturer may complete your order in a week or two, but you also need to consider how long it will take for the order to reach you and the shipping method.

Chapter 9: How You Can Find the Best Deals

There are several ways to find the best deals when sourcing for products, but this chapter will provide you the best methods for sourcing.

1. Clearance aisles. These can be great places to find the best deals on products, so try not to ignore them. You can find over there products with huge discounts, so they can be used to your advantage. The main idea behind this method is to find products at incredibly low prices and sell them at a price much higher on Amazon or other sales channels. It's really not mandatory to source for products online; you can be amazed by what deals you can find at physical stores. You can get a great deal if you check for products at a local drugstore, where can be found some clearances. There are huge retailers in the United States that have clearance aisles at the back of the store. You probably will not sell on Amazon drugs that you found in the clearance section at Walgreens, but still, you can find some pretty interesting offers back there. There are special aisles at stores like Walmart and Walgreens that sell products on clearance. Check the products displayed over there — you might be surprised to find not only incredibly low prices but also diversity. This is why the clearance section is a must for you in order to find out the best deals out there.

2. *Liquidation or surplus stores.* It's true that every niche of products has its traits, and among these traits, the profit margin is definitely one of the most important traits. If you do want to operate in the "health and beauty product" niche category, you will find out that discontinued products can be very profitable. The explanation is very simple. When a person is used with the same beauty product, they are willing to pay some extra money in order to buy that beauty product again. To speculate this fact, you can hold on to your inventory for a longer period of time, just enough time to ask for a premium price. This seems to be a more advanced and complicated thing to do, but just consider this thing — you can buy a product at a discounted price of 75% off, and you can have the opportunity to sell it at double or triple the price. Now that's a profit margin that should make you start thinking about where to find the same product at the same price to sell at that premium price.

But let's try to understand how these liquidation stores work. When the chain stores have some discontinued products, they first place it in the clearance section. If they don't sell, the products are sent to a centralized location and then handed over to the liquidation stores. So if you didn't find anything too interesting at your local Walmart or

Walgreens, you might need to check next the liquidation stores.

Products in liquidation stores are sold with 50–70% off from the original retail price, and there are plenty of these offers, so you are not limited to one shelf or one aisle in the back of your local store. You can find a store full of products at this huge discounted price. The need for a specific product can make your customers pay more than they used to. When you go to these liquidation stores, you will not shop for a tube of toothpaste or a shower gel. You are not buying things for your own use, so you need to be prepared to spend a lot of money on inventory that you will eventually sell on Amazon. A shopping campaign of $2,000–$3,000 can easily provide you profits of $10,000 — a profit that can be obtained over the year, so not quite immediately.

These first two methods showed you methods to source for products in physical locations, where you can easily get the merchandise, so you don't have to ship it to your address.

3. *Online sourcing.* Merchants often refer to sourcing online as *online arbitrage*. It's not because you don't have the time anymore for sourcing products in physical locations (retail arbitrage), but it's important to use any tool you have at your disposal. Therefore, you have to diversify and avoid using just one method for sourcing products — use them all. When you source for products online, you can extend your search to different locations. Perhaps there are better deals elsewhere. Don't let the distance scare you off. There are plenty of merchants sourcing for products from China, and they run a very profitable operation, taking into consideration the profit margin that these products can provide. When you source online, you have to think about shipping too. So in order to make this process worth it, you will need to buy a massive quantity (in bulk).

4. *BOLO mastermind tips.* BOLO stands for "be on the lookout" and represents tips from other merchants. I know what you are thinking now — you are probably wondering why other merchants would like to help you. They might be your competitors, but they can also treat you with respect. Some of them may be from your own network (since you have to create your very own network in order to expand your relationships), and they can help you find products easier. They can encourage you to get a product from suppliers because it's making them a huge profit. The BOLOMart is a network of merchants gathered just for one purpose — to get new insights about where to find the best deals for sourcing and to provide their own source to other interested merchants. It's a give-and-take system that can work wonders for different sellers out there.

***

These are just some places where you can find some very interesting deals. When it comes to the methods you can use, you have three primary options: (1) DIY products, (2) manufacturer or wholesaler, and (3) dropshipping. Let's try to get some more details regarding each option.

DIY products involve crafting, so you will have to be a very good craftsman. Handmade products are becoming more and more popular despite the times we are living in. Industrial products are made for consumerism, so they are deliberately made to break easier. The quality of their parts is not that good simply because the manufacturing process is made that way. The point is, when the product breaks, just buy a new one. Handmade products tend to last a lot more and have a better quality than industrial ones. In most cases, handmade products are more expensive than industrial ones, but this is absolutely normal. However, you will still have to face some challenges, like sourcing materials (you can use flea markets, estate sales, different retailers, craft stores, or friends and family), hiring a carrier, and learning how to use packaging for your products — plus you will need to estimate how long it will take to make your products, find a place where you can store your products, and know the timeline required for making the products.

When you simply don't have the skills or conditions to make your own product, then you will need to hire those who can do it for you — **manufacturers or**

wholesalers. The process involves creating and developing products on an industrial scale. The whole sourcing process is the same one as mentioned in the previous chapter when you source for products in the Chinese market using the Alibaba platform.

Another option you probably never thought of is ***dropshipping***, which literally means buying from a vendor and listing their products directly in your online store. You will need to pay for your order, and the vendor will do the shipping part on your behalf. In this case, you will need to check more vendors, find as many references about them as you can, evaluate the options correctly, ask for samples, and choose the vendor with the best samples.

To maximize the sourcing process, you will need to pick one method and try to use all of the possible places you can think of to source for products. I would highly recommend that you go for the manufacturer/wholesaler option, as you should dedicate your time to find new and innovative ways to sell your products to your customers. You don't want to work way too hard on the crafting and have no time to work on your product listing, description, title, SEO techniques, and advertising campaigns.

Chapter 10: Set Your Own Alerts

In the sourcing process, you will need to develop your own network of manufacturers and suppliers and keep an eye on them all the time. The success of your business depends on how well the sourcing and the acquisition process goes, as everything related to them needs to be cost-effective. If you want to have the best profit margin out there, then you need to get the best deals you can possibly have related to the products you want to sell. Your competitors may be getting their products from the same wholesalers or manufacturers, so when the supplier has some interesting offers, it's important to seize the deals before anyone else.

Picture it like this! You already have a list of suppliers and manufacturers that you are working with, but you still want to know when they have special offers or discounts, as you definitely like to take advantage of the opportunity and buy as many products as possible (when I say as much as possible, keep in mind the storage factor and, if you are using FBA, how fast you can turn over the inventory, as you don't want to pay that much for storage costs). This will create an extra advantage for you because you might benefit more from an offer than your competitors.

You will have smaller sourcing costs, which will lead to more leverage when it comes to the price you want to sell your products. Your competitors may not have this advantage, so they can't lower the price as much as you can, as there will be no longer a profit margin for them. Therefore, getting the products at a lower price than your competitors will increase your profit margin and leave you more space to play with your price. Your competitors may not have this advantage, so this is the "ace up your fields."

Now you are probably wondering how you can seize these deals before anyone else. The trick is to always keep an eye on the offers from your suppliers. Ask them to send you a notification every time there is a special offer for their products. You can receive a newsletter from them regarding the latest offers, or you can check their social media page — usually, all companies post their latest news in there. If you have your suppliers or manufacturers on Facebook, you will receive a notification every time they post something new. Their posts can be about the latest offers or different kinds of announcements.

Additionally, you can use some very interesting sourcing tools with the Google Chrome browser, and these extensions will keep an eye on the manufacturers, suppliers, or products that you want to buy. When there is something new, you will be notified immediately so that you don't have to browse again to find the latest offers. Such notifications and alerts will inform you immediately after an offer is posted, so you can jump on it if it's interesting enough for you.

Do you want to have an unbeatable price on the sales channel that you are activating? Getting the product at a lower price than your competition will definitely give you the extra advantage, so that's why setting up the alerts will help you get the best deals before your competitors do. They may not have the same costs as you. Probably they don't pay the same fee for fulfillment services, or they don't pay the same price for getting the products delivered to them and may have fewer sales channels than you, hence fewer places to sell the products.

Obviously, the more you buy, the better price you will get. So try to establish the best relations with the suppliers and manufacturers from your list — you want to be notified immediately about their special offers. Moreover, you definitely should be close enough to them for you to get preferential discounts. This is how you can lower the acquisition price so that you can focus on your profit margin. It all depends on how you do your math, as you already know how much you pay for shipping. Hopefully you will turn the inventory around fast enough so that you don't have to worry about increased storage fees. Without any doubt, the acquisition costs play a decisive role in settling the retail price (the price you are using to sell the product on your sales channels), but the volume of sales can get you the handsome profits that you want.

Chapter 11: Using Email Lists

Sourcing is important because it will help you find great deals of the product you are looking for. When sourcing, you need to consider every possible method or source for great deals. One way to go is to build a database of wholesalers that are close to your location. Depending on the area where you live, you can have many or few wholesalers. If you've already made up your mind about the product you want to sell, it's important to find wholesalers that are specialized in that product. You will need to compile a list of your potential wholesalers, with all the details you need (address, contact person, phone number, and email address). You will need to approach them, introduce yourself, and let them know what products you are interested in. Therefore, send emails to all of the wholesalers in your list, introducing yourself and describing your company. Mention what you are looking for and inquire about your products of interest. Most wholesalers are very interested in getting a new customer, so they will reply promptly enough, and perhaps you can even schedule a meeting for you to check the inventory that the wholesaler has.

Although you can end up ordering products from a wholesaler without even having to visit them, it's better to pay them a visit if you can, as this can help you a lot to find out what kind of people you are dealing with, to check the storage conditions, and most of all, to check the product itself. See if the product is what you need. Check its quality. Test it if possible. If you like what you see (that is, the product is according to your requirements and meets your expectations), then it's best to move on to discuss terms and negotiate the price per unit and other important details related to your collaboration, like discount offered for ordering a higher quantity.

If you are proactive and reach out to the wholesalers that you are interested in, they will add you to their database, and you can receive notifications when new inventory is available or when there are special discounts applied, depending on the volume of sales.

Chapter 12: Timing Your Niche Market

The success of your business can be seriously influenced by the market you are activating in. This is all about choosing where to operate. If you want to sell the most popular product, there are plenty of other merchants already doing what you want to do, and imposing yourself on such a market is very difficult. You need to focus on finding a niche where you can easily grow and impose yourself as a major player in the market. The niche market is about finding opportunities, so you will need to study the market, split the market into several segments, and find out which product is preferred by each segment.

When you notice that some specific products or services are unmet, you need to understand that this will be your entry into this market. That's the product you will need to deliver in order to become the king of this market. Small businesses are a lot more flexible than big companies, and they can easily adapt if they want to sell products. On top of that, these small companies can even dominate the niche market, taking advantage of the big company's inability to adapt and be more flexible. In order to rule a niche market with absolute authority, you will need to consider the following tips:

1. Provide a unique product or service. The ideal situation is to be the only one selling a specific product. However, this product will have to satisfy the unmet needs of the customers of this market. Make sure that your products can have a high demand and then prepare to sell.

2. Provide a marketable service or product. What's the point of coming up with a very innovative product if no one cares about it or if it doesn't help customers with anything? In order to provide a product that can sell, you will need to spot the needs of your potential customers. You will need to conduct a comprehensive market research study in order to discover these needs and come up with the product that best suits those needs. You can even prelaunch your products and ask for feedback from different people using this constructive criticism to improve your products. So make sure that there is an obvious need for your product; otherwise, it will not sell.

3. Select an available niche market. Let's be clear! There isn't enough space for too many players on one market. Before even starting your business or trying to come up with the product you want to sell, you will need to select the market you want to activate in. You need to look for potential competitors, and if you can find the right market with no competition at all (all insignificant competition), make sure you own the market.

4. *Market, market, market.* Because your brand awareness is kind of low, you will need to apply some marketing techniques in order to make your brand known by other people. The success of your business can depend on the connection you are trying to make with the target segment of people. If you are able to connect with it and make the people of this market understand why they need the product, then you are in for a good start. Otherwise, you will need to find a different approach. Advertising may be important, but it can fail to explain why people really need your product. On the other hand, marketing can educate any potential customers you might have. Once you can build a relationship with them, you can contact them on a regular basis, and you can make them understand why they need the product.

By applying all these tips, you can end up owning your niche market and mastering it. So you are the one calling the shots on it and take most of the benefits from it.

As a newbie to the world of online sales, you will need to find your spot on a niche market, as you can't even dream of competing with giant players in "the big league." Finding your niche market is an essential factor to your business, and this aspect can have a powerful impact on the success of your business. In order to succeed with your online sales business, you will need to respect the following things:

- Make sure you deliver products or services that customers need.

- Offer a superior customer support service than your competitors.

Chapter 13: Take Advantage of Price Coupons, Rebates, and Cashbacks

Nothing can attract more customers like rebates, cashbacks, and price coupons. These kinds of marketing strategies can attract customers like crazy. Showing a flat price may not attract customers; however, when you display the price of the product above the old price (which is higher than the new one) with a red line in the middle of it, this will suggest a discount.

Although you are sourcing for products, you can still have the same behavior, just like end consumers when they are faced with promotions. If you can get an even better deal on the products that you want to source, why not benefit from all these forms of promotions? Even wholesalers have valid reasons to run promotional campaigns. The end goal is to increase sales and turn around some inventory. Discounts are usually the most common promotion sales; however, there are a lot more options for promotions, as wholesalers and retailers are very inventive when it comes to this aspect of the business. Some other ways of promotions include price coupons, rebates, and cashbacks. But let's get through these last methods to better understand what they mean and how you can benefit from it.

A very used promotion method is the price coupon. This represents a document, a piece of paper that shows you are entitled to get a discount for the goods shown on this coupon. It can be a percentage discount or a fixed amount in monetary units. Price coupons can be found in newspapers or magazines, as they are shown in there as a form of advertisement. Price coupons can also be found in leaflets, internet ads, and so on. Although huge chains of fast-food restaurants are using price coupons, they can be found for other purposes as well.

Advantages of discount coupons:

- They can induce first-time purchase.
- They can make for the seller additional profits.

Disadvantages of discount coupons:

- They usually cause occasional sales only.

Rebates are considered amounts of money paid as a return, reduction, or refund. Perhaps the most common form of rebates is the mail-in rebate (MIR), which requires the buyer to send a coupon or a barcode in order to get a check for a specific amount, depending on the product he wants to buy. This form of promotion is widely used by different fast-food chains, supermarkets, banks, airlines, or retail stores. When it comes to advantages and disadvantages, they are about the same, just like the other forms of promotion.

Cashbacks is a promotion form that allows you to receive some money back in cash after purchasing a product. Some buyers are simply fanatic about cashbacks, and they are using special apps to find these cashbacks and benefit from them.

Some of the most popular apps for finding rewards and cashbacks are as follows:

- Drop

- Swagbucks

- Bitwalking

- Mobee

- Belly

- Fronto

- Cosign

- iBotta

- Shopkick

- Checkout 51

Some promotions can also be used for massive inventories of the same product, so you might need to keep an eye on them on the internet or on the apps you can use for finding promotions.

Chapter 14: Don't Miss Any Liquidation

Sourcing doesn't have to be solely an online activity, as you can still go out there and find extraordinary deals, depending on the products that you want to sell. Some of the great deals can be found locally, in your city, so you don't have to search online for products in the Chinese market — unless you really want to. Sourcing is perhaps the most important part of retail arbitrage, as it scans the market for great deals related to the products you wish to sell.

When stores want to clear their stock of some products, they can organize clearance sales, wherein they offer huge discounts just to lure people into buying the product with a huge discount. A very interesting case is discontinued products that are no longer being promoted by stores, and they just sit somewhere in the back of the store, where there is minimum visibility, so the buyers do not quite see these kinds of products.

There are plenty of retailers who have a clearance section in their shops, so you might want to check it out. It can be only a shelf or just a corner inside a store, but it's still worth checking it. If clearance products are not being sold, they are centralized and sent over to liquidation stores, as this could be the last chance for these products to be sold. Liquidation stores can be found in different cities throughout America, and they can offer pretty impressive deals on wholesale products. You can buy products at even 70% discount, so you can sell them at a much higher price on Amazon or eBay.

Wholesaling can be a tough business. Some of the suppliers may end up having a large number of products that apparently no one wants to buy. These wholesalers can be quite close to your location, so it's highly recommended to drive over there and check the inventory they have. Wholesalers will use every possible method at their disposal to advertise the liquidation of their stock, so most likely, you will not be the only person who knows about the liquidation. You don't have to go far to get to a liquidation store — you can still find great deals locally. Therefore, look for your local wholesalers and try to have a special relationship with them — perhaps you can even have an extra advantage.

You might find about the liquidation before your competitors or get other benefits from the wholesaler, like preferential discounts. This special relationship can only be built over time when you order loads of products from your wholesaler. So make sure you have your alerts on so you won't miss any liquidation.

Use Craigslist, eBay community, or social media to find out about the liquidations from your preferred wholesalers. In order to seize the opportunity, you will need to act fast, as time can cost you money. If you delay your action, your competition can get there before you and take the most benefits from the current liquidation. Many sellers are not aware of these opportunities, or there might by a misbelief that these products have very low quality and nobody wants them. You don't have to think like that. The truth is, you can still find amazing deals with liquidations — you only have to be persistent. Don't consider this method of sourcing as a waste of time, because if you are persistent enough, it will totally pay off one day.

Chapter 15: Some of the Best Places to Source (eBay, Craigslist)

There are plenty of merchants out there who prefer to source for products on the Chinese market only, so Alibaba is the heaven of manufacturers and suppliers. They think that's the place to be if they want to source for products. While most merchants are very satisfied with the companies they deal with from the Chinese market, some sellers are a bit reluctant when it comes to dealing with such companies. It's not that they think that they can only get poor-quality products, but they prefer less hassle, so they simply don't want anything to do with imports.

If everyone would source for products directly on the Chinese market, there wouldn't be any wholesaler anywhere else but in China. Note that import taxes from China tend to increase, so sourcing from China may not be as attractive as it used to be. Also, you still need to consider the shipping time and how long it will take to process your order. You simply won't have the products you ordered in one week, as perhaps only the manufacturing part is done in this period. You will also need to consider the shipping process. What delivery method will you use (cargo plane or by sea), and how much will you need to pay for this process? For all these companies, there are local wholesalers that can provide you interesting deals without having to contact companies all the way from China. Some online platforms like eBay or Craigslist can provide you with interesting options when it comes to sourcing for products online.

eBay seems to be a proper environment to gather plenty of wholesalers from different domains of activity. The eBay community has a pretty impressive list of wholesale deals, so you might need to check them also. After all, it's better to check all possible sources before deciding where you want to source the product from. As you already know, eBay is famous for auctions, so why not auction for wholesale products? There are still plenty of wholesalers present on this platform, so why not source for products in here? You can get quite good deals on this website, which is already used by so many people worldwide.

eBay can make you think again if you want to source for products in China (Alibaba), which involves going through all the hassle of shipping the products overseas, customs, import taxes, and so on. Why would you like to experience anything like this when you can find decent offers in the United States? eBay is also a great platform to check the trending products, so when you do your market research on the most popular products out there, you might also want to consider this platform, not just Amazon.

You can find which product category is among the most popular ones. You can also check for the most popular products in there and the key players for every category. The research process is very similar to the one on Amazon, but in order to have more ideas about the ideal product you would like to sell, it is better to check more sources.

eBay's popularity is decreasing slowly, so it can no longer give Amazon a run for its money, but this doesn't mean that the platform has lost its charm and utility. There are still plenty of buyers online who prefer this platform, so you would have to check the latest trends on eBay. Find out the products that are selling like hotcakes and see if these products can inspire you what products to sell. Plus, you can always consider eBay as one of your sales channels (more details on this in a later chapter).

The internet can provide you endless opportunities when it comes to selling online, including many websites that you can use for sourcing your products or to sell them. Craigslist is also a very popular website in the United States, although it looks like a very rudimental website for ads. However, there is a lot more than meets the eye, as this website is one of the most useful ones you can use in the United States. Probably, not too many merchants consider this Craigslist when it comes to sourcing their products.

You can find below some of the main reasons why you should still consider this platform to source for the products you want to sell. Craigslist is considered one of the most interesting sources of local products that are very cheap or possibly even free. The Craigslist app can easily spot those offers, so you should consider getting this app on your smartphone to search for new inventory every time you can. You can use this app to set your own alerts based on the keywords you enter, therefore notifying you when there is an inventory available that might interest you.

To make the most out of using this app, there are a few steps to follow:

1. Download the app for your phone. You can find it for both iOS and Android users. There is a free version and a paid one. To get just the basic features, the free app is more than enough. However, if you do want to get the full features, you might need to consider getting the paid version — it's just $ 2.99, by the way.

2. Choose the city or cities you want.

3. Look for the "For Sale" section. In this section, you will find items that are on sale and possibly even for free.

4. Browse for the products that interest you the most. The products are categorized to make them easier to be found by you.

5. Check the "free" section as well. This section will probably amaze you, as you will see plenty of people giving away a lot of items they don't need anymore.

6. Before making an offer to a Craigslist seller, you might want to check if you can find the same product on eBay and Amazon. Compare the prices of the products sold on these two platforms and then approach the Craigslist seller to receive an offer for his inventory.

As already mentioned, you can set the app to provide you alerts when the product you are looking for become available on Craigslist. These alerts are based on the keywords you entered. You can easily notice if an item is sold for more on Amazon or eBay, so you definitely need to be notified of any of these listings. The app will also allow you to sort your criteria or to display products with photos only, so you find exactly what to look for. If you find something very interesting, you can easily make the call from the app without having to copy down the phone number of the seller, making this process a lot faster and simpler.

Keep in mind that products on Craigslist are often sold at a lower price than they are usually sold online. The whole purpose of the website is to provide convenient sales, so if you want to sell for profits, this is not the site for you. Buyers already know this detail, and they are using it for their advantage. Some of the main reasons why you should use Craigslist are (1) this platform doesn't involve any shipping and (2) transactions are made very fast. A seller can post their listings on this platform, and if someone buys the inventory, they will need to pay in cash, which can provide the seller the extra guarantee they want related to buyers. Also, this aspect will lower the prices for the inventory. If you browse through the product categories of this website, you will find plenty of products that are given away for free or sold at a low price.

If you do want to find very popular products (with high demand), Craigslist is not the site for you, but the deals you can find here will definitely make you consider it for sourcing purposes. The profitability of your sourcing activity is determined by the price you want to sell the product on your sales channel (whether it's Amazon, eBay, or your own website). Obviously, if you already know the popular products on these platforms and have conducted market research on the product you want to sell, the market, and the key players operating in this market, you will know what products you will need to source on Craigslist. The deals you will find here are simply great, but you will also be very careful with the products you receive. You will need to make sure that the products are in good condition. Only if you really need the products and if they are free, you should accept them in bad condition.

Craigslist is an excellent place to find deals, but when you use it for sourcing products, you might want to consider the following tips:

- If a seller doesn't seem to be trustworthy, move on.

- If you do want to do in-person transactions, you might want to take a friend with you. If you plan to go all by yourself, try to meet the seller in a well-trafficked public spot during daylight to check the products. Some police stations from the United States even provide their own parking lot for Craigslist exchanges.

- If you don't want to use the Craigslist app, you might want to consider the IFTTT.com to receive the alerts you want for products being on sale on the Craigslist platform.

- Make sure you check Craigslist and similar websites very often. New products may be listed quite frequent.

Chapter 16: The Right Way to Source/Make Purchases

As you probably know, when you start your financial projection about profits, a very important fact you will need to consider is the price of the acquisition. This aspect will determine your profit margin, as you simply can't sell a product lower than the price you used to pay for it. Companies worldwide have procurement departments and use the latest tools and software to find out the best deals out there. At the end of the day, it all comes down to one thing — profit. When you sell a product, do not simply rely on one channel only. We are not living in the '60s, and customers have so many options to consider when buying a product. You need to be easily found. That's why merchants nowadays sell through multiple channels. Can you imagine a merchant selling products these days just through their very limited brick-and-mortar store? They will definitely not sell too much, and their sales will go down until they have to close the shop eventually as they can no longer afford to keep it open.

Although e-commerce didn't replace traditional stores, this type of retail is growing incredibly fast, just like wildfire. For 2020, it's expected that global e-commerce sales will reach $4 trillion, according to eMarketer. The way to survive in this very competitive market is to sell products through multiple channels. This is how you can maximize your sales. The same goes for product sourcing. You will need to source products through multiple channels, so don't rely on just one channel. If you sell through multiple channels, you will reach out to more customers. When you source products through different channels, it's very likely to get in touch with a lot more suppliers and manufacturers.

In order to source properly, you will need to respect the following steps:

- Find the most popular products to sell online.

- Validate the idea.

- Find your suppliers or manufacturers.

But first things first — let's take them one by one. The internet can easily provide us the solution for the first step as it's packed with information you can use. In this case, there are a few websites you can check in order to find out the most popular products. Some specialists would agree that the best sources for finding popular products are the following:

- Reddit

- Alibaba

- Flippa

- Alltop

- Amazon

- eBay

Of course, this is just an opinion by some of the specialists in e-commerce. Others may have a more extensive list. However, there are some key factors you will need to consider when choosing the right product for you. These criteria will definitely rule out some of the products displayed in there as possible, but if you do want to be a successful merchant, the ideal product has to meet the following requirements:

1. To be deliverable. When you are selling products online, you have to deal with shipping. The product has to be shippable in a safe manner. Also, the shipping service for it doesn't have to be expensive at all. I guess this criterion rules out fragile products, as well as really heavy and big ones. As you can imagine, the courier will charge you per size of the parcel and for its weight, so you might want to consider this when you sell products online.

2. To be sourceable. What is the point of selling a product online if you can't find it at any supplier or manufacturer? One of the most important rules of selling products online is to find products that can be sourced. You are not a merchant if you are selling something extremely rare (possibly for a large amount of money) but can't find the same product again (or a similar one) to sell on a continuous basis. Extremely rare products are very hard to get, and if you can get your hands on such a product, you will need to pay a fortune on it. You should only pay a fortune for a product that you intend to keep, not sell back immediately, hoping for a better price.

3. *To be year-round.* Try to avoid selling seasonal products, as you want your business to run perfectly all year round, not just for a few months. Boosted sales in the season will not keep your business running for the whole year.

Let's say that you already have something in mind when it comes to the products you want to sell. Now that you have a shortlist of them, you need to move on to the next phase — to validate your idea. This is why you need to ask yourself the following questions:

- Is the demand sufficient for this product?

- What about the competitors? How many are they and how much do they sell?

- Can your product bring more value to the market?

To get answers to these questions, you have to look no further than the Amazon platform. You will need to find a product on this platform, and check the available data for it. Amazon can give you the tools to get all this information, so you can use it to project your sales every month. The data will easily allow you to check the demand and opportunity for every product you plan to sell.

There are even third-party apps or browser extensions that can help you with this task. You are probably asking yourself, How do you know when you set your mind on a good product? It depends on the product category, but some specialists would agree that this product should be selling 300–400 items per month per seller. It's highly important to estimate the volume of sales correctly in order to calculate your estimated profits properly.

However, it's a bit premature to discuss profits when you haven't even sourced the product yet. If you want to calculate your profit margins, you will need to know the retail price (the one you want to use to sell the product) and the acquisition cost (the price per unit you will pay to the supplier or manufacturer). However, that's not all — there are other aspects you will need to consider when trying to figure out your profit. This is why you will need to consider the following aspects:

- What will be the expected price for the product?

- Have you ever considered to import your merchandise if you source the products in a foreign country?

- How much will it cost you to ship your product to customers?

- Can you think of any other costs — e.g., custom taxes, etc.?

- If you want to use Amazon FBA, do you know how much all possible fees will cost?

- If you have your own storage space, do you know how much they will reflect on the cost of your product?

Answering these questions will narrow down your list to just a few products. You will need to study your competition. You need to find out every possible detail about your competitor. There are many details you will need to focus on — not just the price of your competition and market share but also the strategies used by your competition. This is the perfect opportunity to have a SWOT analysis. Use Google to start your market research. Search on Amazon. Use as many tools you can possibly think of in order to get more accurate data regarding your competition.

When you already know what to sell and have information about your competition and the costs of handling your products (storage, shipping, fulfillment costs on Amazon when necessary, possible import costs, and so on), it's time to solve the last piece of the puzzle in the sourcing process, which is to find your suppliers or manufacturers.

Amazon may be a great source of suppliers, but the popular trend is to head over to the Chinese market. Alibaba is perhaps the best platform to search for suppliers or manufacturers. This platform represents the "middle man" between Chinese suppliers and manufacturers and the rest of the companies from all around the world. Alibaba filters the companies present on this platform, as every Chinese supplier and manufacturer displayed on this platform is legit and all of them can communicate in English.

Another excellent website for finding suppliers or manufacturers is Global Sources. This website also opens up the Chinese market to the rest of the world, and it's very similar to Alibaba. You can find excellent deals on the Chinese market, so it's totally worth it to source for products in China, regardless of customs and import taxes or the longer time for shipping.

Communication is the key to successful sourcing, as these platforms can offer the perfect interface between you and the Chinese suppliers or manufacturers. There is a direct messaging option on this platform, but you can also email them directly. Direct messaging is a lot more effective to get things done as you can discuss all the details you need to know in an effective manner and use the emails for official correspondence to confirm your discussions or to exchange official documents like contracts, invoices, or orders. Make sure you confirm your requirements with the manufacturer or supplier and also discuss terms of delivery. When you reach out to them, there are some important guidelines you will need to follow, as you can see below:

- Be as simple and concise as possible.

- Ask all possible questions to get all the information you need to know.

- Find out some rough indicators about costs and production times.

- Be professional but use a friendly tone.

- If you are just starting your business, don't mention this to the supplier or manufacturer. Tell them that you want your product to be a bestseller.

- A picture can say a thousand words, so make sure you exchange photos of the desired product to make sure that you are on the same page with them.

One of the best ways to find suppliers or manufacturers is trade shows. You can search for trade shows relevant to your product on websites like expodatabase.com, fita.org, or 10times.org and find out who attends these trade shows, what products are displayed, when they are organized, and how to visit them. If you want to source products from China, you don't have to fly all over to China to physically meet your potential suppliers and manufacturers. You can use Alibaba or Global Source, but if China comes to you (Chinese suppliers and manufacturers attending a trade show), then you should totally visit the trade show and check the manufacturers or suppliers attending there. It's very good for your business to personally know your business partner. What better way to start a collaboration with these Chinese companies than to meet their representatives in person at these trade shows?

If you ever wonder what the ideal supplier or manufacturer needs to have, you might want to check the list below:

- They have strong communication and language skills (they have to be able to communicate fluently in English).

- They have experience in manufacturing/supplying your product.

- They are flexible to manufacture the product the way you want.

- They can easily agree with your price range.

- They are eager to start a partnership and to be cooperative.

There are some strong signals that should push you away from these kinds of suppliers or manufacturers.

- They are new in this business.

- They have no experience with the product type that you want.

- Prices are either too high or too low.

\-   They are not too cooperative or responsive.

Chapter 17: Amazon FBA — How to Benefit from It

Amazon is a retailer that doesn't need any introduction, at least not in the civilized world. It is available in just a few countries worldwide like Australia, Brazil, Canada, China, France, Germany, India, Japan, Mexico, Netherlands, Spain, Turkey, United Arabian Emirates, United Kingdom, and the United States. However, their shoppers are not limited just to these countries, as Amazon has customers from plenty of countries worldwide. But this is less important, as there are other stats that are very important for Amazon. At the moment, it's believed that Amazon's e-commerce market has exceeded 50% just in the United States, so Amazon sells more than all its other three main competitors together — eBay, Apple, and Walmart. When you think of online sales, you can't help not thinking about Amazon. The following stats are related to the previous year, and keep in mind that the actual stats are even more in favor of Amazon. Let's check them below:

1. When it comes to checking the price of a product, 9 out of 10 consumers are doing it on Amazon.

2. 2% of Echo owners have bought a product via Alexa.

3. There are more than 12 million products sold on Amazon.

4. More than 1.1 million home improvement products are being sold on Amazon.

5. Just in the United States, more than 95 million people are Amazon Prime members.

6. The average amount of money spent per year by an Amazon Prime member is $1.4K.

7. FBA can lead to a 30–50% increase in sales for different merchants.

8. There were more than 5 billion items dispatched by Amazon worldwide in 2017.

9. More than half of the sales made on Amazon are done by third-party sellers.

10. Out of the third-party sellers, around 80% of them sell on other platforms than Amazon.

Speaking of third-party sellers, as you already know, there isn't just Amazon selling on this platform, which is, in fact, a marketplace. There are approximately 2 million resellers worldwide, and their number is growing fast. The most advantageous method to sell on Amazon is its own fulfillment program, Amazon FBA. From these 2 million sellers,

66% of them use the fulfillment services provided by Amazon; the rest of them prefer to use the fulfillment-by-merchant (FBM) method.

FBM doesn't provide too many advantages for the seller, as it makes them responsible for creating the product listings and handling customer support service. They are also in charge of picking, packing, labeling products, and shipping them. In terms of costs, this method is affordable, as they don't have too much money to Amazon, but instead, they will need to support all the expenses for the services they want to use.

On the other hand, Fulfillment by Amazon provides plenty of services for the sales and the after-sale process. This company has plenty of warehouses all over the world that are called fulfillment centers. These centers can provide logistics space for the inventory of merchants. Most of these warehouses were built recently, and they can offer the best conditions for storing merchandise. Therefore, any merchant determined to sell on Amazon can now fully benefit from the outstanding conditions offered by these fulfillment centers and from the best services this company has to offer. As a merchant, you can associate your name with Amazon by selling on their marketplaces, sharing its success. Over 2 million resellers are already doing this, selling around half of the products on this platform. The majority of these merchants are using the FBA program because of the following reasons:

- It allows them to store their merchandise in an Amazon Fulfillment Center.

- Amazon handles the picking, packing, and shipping of products to the final customer.

- The merchants will get the customer support service done by Amazon, and they are famous for providing the best service (although it refers just to tracking, returns, or refunds).

- Your products are visible to Prime members, who usually spend a lot more money on Amazon than usual customers.

You can imagine that Amazon doesn't provide all these services for free; they don't just give it away. You can opt for different types of accounts in order to find out the prices for these services. This is what is covered by the fulfillment services, but the storage services are calculated separately. It depends on how much your inventory stays in a warehouse. This is a cost that you need to pay close attention, as it can determine whether selling on Amazon is for you or not. In order to use this method, there are some requirements to be met, but you also need to estimate your expenses in order to establish whether this service is for you or not.

Let me break it down for you what Amazon can do for a reseller if the merchant chooses the FBA option:

- It receives the inventory in one of its fulfillment centers. There are more than 100 huge warehouses just in the United States, some of them having more than 1,000,000 square feet (Wallace et al., 2019). Therefore, you can find a lot of storage for your inventory in one of these warehouses. You will need to let Amazon know what kind of product you are sending, and they will let you know where you can send it.

- It can sort and store your goods. Upon receiving your products, Amazon will organize and place them in the right areas of the fulfillment center. You simply can't imagine better storing conditions for your merchandise, as it's safely stored inside these warehouses. If your products get damaged during the storage process, Amazon will reimburse completely the value of the merchandise.

Let's just say that all of these aspects caught your attention and you are seriously thinking about selling your products on Amazon. As a word of advice: you will need to use different marketing strategies to advertise your goods and monitor your inventory constantly. Speaking about your inventory, take a look below to understand what you need to consider:

- How fast can your product be sold? Bear in mind that there are some storage fees you will need to consider. Therefore, if your products don't sell fast enough, you will need to pay higher storage fees.

- Think about your profit margin. As you probably know, this is what you can use to pay all the fees required. If you consider this aspect properly, chances are that you can also keep some money after paying all the fees.

- Check your Amazon account on a regular basis, as you will need to keep an eye on your inventory on a daily basis.

- Use the right marketing techniques to make your sales go through the roof and to make your products a lot more visible for the rest of the consumers using this platform. Just imagine the competition when your products are displayed alongside 350,000,000 products on Amazon. Clearly, you will need to find ways in order to make your product stand out from the crowd.

Benefits of Using Amazon FBA

It's really hard to think of any other method that can boost sales for merchants as Amazon FBA does. If you want your products to be available for more than 400 million potential buyers (Smith, 2019), you should definitely choose this option. But before you do that, you will need to understand the benefits of choosing this method.

1. Easy delivery and logistics services. If you are a merchant and you are determined to do the whole fulfillment process, you need to know that it is very time-consuming, and it gets even worse when you have a very high number of orders. You will be handling all the shipping, packing, and labeling for all the customers, and you will be losing a serious amount of time instead of spending this time on something extremely important, like marketing strategies. This is where Amazon FBA can step in and take the whole fulfillment process out of your hands. By choosing this option, you can externalize storage, picking, packing, labeling, and shipping the product to the customer. This should give you plenty of time to take advantage of this platform while you apply the most appropriate and effective marketing techniques.

2. Decreased shipping fees. When you want to do the whole fulfillment process all by yourself, you will need to know exactly what you are up against and what you are dealing with. You are a small merchant that can only send a few tens or hundreds of items per month, so you need to find a very good contract for shipping services. Amazon, on the other hand, has more negotiation power and extraordinary deals when it comes to shipping services. They can negotiate on your behalf the best courier services you can possibly have out there if you choose the FBA method.

3. *Amazon handles your returns.* You can expect that on Amazon, customers come first, so you will have to expect a higher number of returns than you usually expect. Handling all the paperwork can give you goosebumps, as all this administrative work is not something too easy. This company can take a load out of your mind and handle this service for you if you are an Amazon FBA user. Amazon can charge you extra for this service, but it can definitely be worthwhile for you.

4. *Excellent customer support service.* Sales are all about getting new customers, but if you want to win their loyalty, then you need extraordinary customer support service. You can benefit from such a service because Amazon will do its best to provide your customers with the best service out there. It can handle this service 24/7 via phone, live chat, or email. However, you need to bear in mind that Amazon's part, in this case, is strictly related to tracking or delivering your products, as well as handling returns or refunds. If a customer wants to find out information about the product, Amazon will notify you, and you need to answer to your customer's queries within 24 hours.

5. *More storage space than you can possibly imagine.* The warehouses provided by Amazon have plenty of space for your merchandise, so you don't have to look for proper warehouses to store your goods. This company can provide the best storing conditions you can find out there, so why not benefit from it and take a serious load off your mind?

6. *Fast delivery*. You can't expect to receive a product you bought on Amazon just as fast as you receive pizza. However, due to its very good contracts with couriers and especially because Amazon has fulfillment centers in several countries around the globe, products can be delivered in a maximum of 48 hours. This estimate is applicable for domestic shipping. International shipping may take a bit longer than that, as the product is being handled by at least two couriers. For domestic shipping, when a customer chooses to buy a product, this is being sent out to them from the closest fulfillment center.

7. Amazon can do the fulfillment process for you, even if you sell your products through other channels. If you sell your products on several other platforms, other marketplaces, or perhaps your own webshop, you are responsible for sending the products to your customers. Well, Amazon can help you here also, as it can offer you the multi-channel fulfillment (MCF) option, putting storage space from its warehouses at your disposal even though the goods you store in there are not for Amazon customers. Such a service can be easily activated, and it provides you information about order updates or tracking for the products.

Disadvantages of Using FBA

If you do choose to use this method, you also need to understand its downside. If you run the math, you might discover that this service is simply not for you, so it's not recommended for everyone. However, in order to take your own decision, you might need to check the information below:

1. This program costs money. When you choose to use FBA, you will need to consider both storage and fulfillment fees. If the expenses are pretty much clear for the fulfillment side, the storage fees are calculated differently. First of all, you need to know how fast your products can sell. Because you are paying for storage space for a period of time, the more your products stay in the warehouse, the more you have to pay. If you can estimate these costs, you will be able to determine the size of your profits.

2. Long-term storage can cost a lot. If your inventory is left in the Amazon fulfillment centers for a very long time (like six months, for instance), you will have to pay extremely high storage fees, so this is something that you definitely need to avoid. Try to sell your merchandise as quickly as possible so you will not have to pay very high storage fees.

3. Expect more returns. For Amazon, customers come first, so this company encourages customers to return a product if they are not satisfied with it. As a seller, you will need to comply with these rules, as they are part of the terms and conditions. To make matters a lot smoother for both customers and sellers, Amazon facilitates the return process and makes it a lot easier. Returns may occur when you are experiencing impulsive or test buying for your customers.

4. It's not easy to prepare a product. Selling on Amazon comes with a very strict set of rules when it comes to labeling and packaging a product. They need to be entered into a database, marked properly, and sent to the right warehouse. It will definitely take some time until you get used to the procedures, but this is something necessary in order to sell on this platform.

5. It's not easy to check for your inventory. Monitoring your remaining stock may not be the easiest thing to do, as you are not able to see the list of your available stock in real-time. However, you can still have a clear idea of the products that are selling and the ones that are not selling. This can be a lot more difficult when you sell on multiple channels.

6. Taxation is complicated. The fun part of doing business in the United States is that every state has its very own taxes, so you may pay a higher tax in one state than in another. Calculating your taxes can be difficult, especially if your business operates in many states. You can have the business in one state, but

Amazon may need to shuffle the merchandise from one state to state, and this can cause confusion. You are probably wondering if you have to collect the sales tax in the state where you have your headquarters or in every state that Amazon operates in. That's why you need the services of skilled accountants or tax advisers who can easily help you with this situation.

7. *There is a risk that your products can be commingled with other ones from other merchants.* When you set the Amazon seller account, the default option is to get your products mixed with others, but this may lead to unpleasant situations like a customer buying your product and receiving something else entirely or a customer receiving a similar product from a different merchant with a significantly lower quality. Your customer might even receive damaged or counterfeit products, but they will have the impression that you sent them these products on purpose. You don't want this to happen. You don't want your products to be mixed with others, as bad reviews spread like wildfire, and this may force Amazon to ban you permanently from this platform. However, there is a solution to this problem — you can label your products correctly.

Most Important Costs and Fees for Using Amazon FBA

The facts above should not discourage you to subscribe to this service, as the sky's the limit when it comes to sales on Amazon. But before you decide, you should know all the facts first. You can find below a list of the most important fees involved in this program.

1. Subscription. This kind of fee depends on the account type you select, and when you plan to sell on this platform, you can choose from the professional or individual account. You can decide on one of these two options by estimating the number of sales you have per month. If you expect less than 40 sales per month, then it's better to choose the individual plan. If you expect way more than that, then it's highly recommended to go for the professional account. For the individual account, the subscription is for free, while for the professional one, the subscription costs $39.99.

2. Pre-item fee. This type of fee can only be applicable for sellers with individual accounts. Bear in mind that this represents $0.99 for every item you sold using this kind of account. If you have a professional account, you will not have to worry about this fee.

3. Referral fee. This type of fee can vary between 6% and 20% (in most cases). There is an exception, though, for Amazon devices, where the referral fee is 45% (Wallace et al., 2019). This payment is strongly associated with the product category, but the most common percentage is 15%. In dollars, the minimum referral fee should be zero or $1; the only items with higher referral fee are jewelry and watches (in this case, the referral fee is $2).

4. Closing fees. These kinds of fees only apply to video games, DVDs consoles, music, videos, and books. They vary between $0.45 and $1.35, depending on the type of shipment, shipment destination, and category.

5. Fulfillment fees. These types of fees are also predictable and can vary depending on the product's weight and dimensions. Such costs can vary from $2.41 to $10, but some prices are going up since last year.

When it comes to selling on Amazon, there a few fees you will need to consider that can be split into four different categories, as seen below:

a) *Direct costs.* In this category, you should be able to find costs related to purchasing of the product and shipping it from the manufacturer to supplier.

b) *Indirect costs.* You can find here a wide range of costs like accounting, tax, insurance, business travel, samples, website development, etc.

c) *Amazon fees*. These are every expense related to Amazon, like fees for closing, sales, returns, referrals, fulfillment, and storage.

d) Costs of dealing with returns.

In order to calculate the profits you can have if you plan to sell on Amazon, you will need to consider all of the costs above and do your math right. You can't estimate too accurately the volume of your sales nor the storage costs, so you need to find a product that sells fast and in large quantities. There are plenty of sellers on Amazon who are making a handsome profit — their products are very successful and appreciated by plenty of online shoppers.

How to Create Your Very Own Amazon Seller Central Account

If you mean business, then this is one of the first questions you need to ask yourself in order to sell on Amazon. Things are not very complicated here, but you still have to go through a checklist in order to get all set up with Amazon.

When creating your account on Amazon (the Seller Central account), you will be prompted to enter some information, such as the following:

1. Business information. Naturally, this field is all about the business name, address, and contact information

2. Email address. You will need to provide a proper email address suitable for your account. If you have any, a business email address would be perfect (name.surname@companydomain.com). Make sure that your email is working because Amazon will contact you immediately to confirm the account.

3. Credit card information. In order to make payments for all the fees you have to pay for Amazon and receive the money from your sales, you will need a valid debit/credit card number. If you provide a wrong card number, Amazon will immediately cancel your registration. Also, make sure that you fill in the correct billing address for the debit/credit card.

4. Phone number. During the registration process, Amazon will also contact you back by phone, so you definitely need to provide the right number; otherwise, Amazon will not be able to reach you during this process

5. Tax ID. Usually, this kind of information is requested for companies within the United States. Companies in Europe have a VAT number to register. This piece of information is vital for the success of your registration. You will be asked to provide details like the company's federal tax ID number (for the United States) or the social security number. Don't worry, Amazon will handle with care your details, so you don't have to worry about your data being shared online. During this step, you will need to fill in the "1099-K Tax Document Interview."

6. *State tax ID.* Mentioning the state (or states) where you operate your business is important in order to get the right state tax ID.

Taxation may become an issue, as you will see, so it's important to get advice from tax specialists or from websites like taxify.com, avalara.com, or taxjar.com.

Questions Amazon Sellers Ask

Truth be told — you can easily provide the information above to create your very own Amazon Seller Central account, you only have to be a bit careful with the data you enter and may need a bit of help when it comes to taxation, but the registration process should not cause you any problems. However, there are still other issues you will need to clarify. That's why you will need to ask yourself the following questions:

1. Where can you send the Amazon order returns?

For Amazon, the customer comes first, so this company is oriented toward achieving customer satisfaction, and they are doing a hell of a job to provide the best customer service experience out there. Part of this service is handling returns, as their customers have the option to return the product for different reasons. If you want to sell on this marketplace, you will need to comply with Amazon's rules, including the one regarding returns. I know you don't want to have returns — no merchant wants that — but your ultimate goal should be customer satisfaction. Returns may occur from time to time, probably more than you expected.

Amazon will do the administrative part for you, but you still have to handle them, so you can do it by yourself or you can do it with the help of a specialized agency like openedboxreturns.com or tradeportc.com. These agencies are specialized in testing and grading returns and placing the products back on sale. For the success of your business, you need to have a designated person to handle all possible customer inquiries. Please be aware that customer queries should be handled within 24 hours. This is not me saying this — it's in fact, Amazon's policy. Therefore, before even setting up your Amazon Seller Central account, you may need to consider someone to do these roles (return and customer queries).

2. Is commingling an option to consider if you choose to use Fulfillment by Amazon (FBA)?

The FBA option will expose your product to prime members and all potential buyers using this platform. You may have more customers than you can ever imagine (hopefully), but the true challenge is making sure your products are delivered to all of your customers. When your products are stored in an Amazon warehouse, there is a risk that your products can get mingled with the ones from other merchants who can sell similar products — or worse, counterfeit versions of your product.

Now imagine the consequences of a customer getting a counterfeit product, thinking that the product they received came from you! Your inventory is sent to a fulfillment center, where it can get mixed with other products from different merchants. Amazon might make the mistake of sending a product to your customer that is not yours. Explaining the situation to your customer is the least of your problems. You can end up with terrible reviews and complaints, so at one point, Amazon may be forced to ban you from this marketplace. It doesn't seem to be your fault, but you are getting the blame for it. Obviously, you don't want anything like that to happen, so you need to find a way for your customer to always receive the product that you are sending, not another merchant.

Fortunately for you, Amazon can provide you the solution in this case, as it all comes down to labeling. When you create your own seller account, the default option for labeling is "stickerless," an option that can easily lead to getting your products mixed with the ones from another seller. At this point of the registration process, you will need to pay extra attention, as you can choose the "stickered" option for your account in order to prevent the mess of mixing your products with others that are not yours. Therefore, make sure you choose this option when creating your account and before sending anything over to a fulfillment center. So why expose yourself to so many risks when you can easily choose the "stickered" option and have an extra guarantee that your products are handled properly and sent to the right customers?

3. Are you thinking of using the "doing business as" (DBA) name for your account?

Amazon can give you the option to hide your business name or merchant identity when selling on this platform. Let's say that you are selling different brands on Amazon. Would you like them to know that you are selling their products? Probably not! This is why you can choose to hide your identity and type in whatever you like in the DBA section.

4. Is your product category permitted on Amazon?

Although Amazon has built a diversified marketplace (so there is a very wide range of products), you simply can't sell anything on this platform. There are some categories that are prohibited in this marketplace. Some good examples would be alcohol, vehicle tires, gift certificates, pamphlets, price tags, or other categories. If you are not selling products from one of these categories, then you are in luck, so nothing should block you from selling on this platform. It's highly recommendable to sell products with high profit margins and those that sell very fast. These two aspects will determine the size of your profits.

Something else you will need to consider is your very own seller catalog on Amazon. The best way to find out which products are popular or not is to add all of your products to your catalog in the first 30 days after opening your account. You can see which products are not selling as they should, so you might have problems with their stock keeping units (SKUs) or brands. If you are experiencing some restrictions from Amazon, you might need to modify your catalog or even to close the account.

Skills for Amazon Sellers

When there are over 2 million sellers on this platform, success is not guaranteed for third-party resellers. As a merchant, you are facing too much competition; however, you can still make a handsome profit if you play your cards right. You will need to have the right skills in order to stand out from the crowd, make your product more visible, and boost your sales.

1. Using Excellent marketing content to compile the best product listings. What are the odds of selling a completely unique product on this platform? In most of the cases, there is at least one competitor for you who sells the exact product or has another one very similar for sale. So can you persuade customers to buy your product, not the one from your competitors? The trick is to optimize the content you have on your page. Focus on the product title and description, generic keywords, and bullet points (all for SEO purposes). Another helpful tip is to add high-quality images, which will have to include a lifestyle photo on the product you have on sale. The images should have a white background and a resolution over 500×500 pixels, without having to place your own watermark on it.

2. Understanding the volume of sales of your product and preventing running out of stock. When you have a product that is becoming quite popular on Amazon, chances are that it will run out of stock at some point. To prevent this from happening, you will need to replenish your inventory. If you are selling products that sell regularly, you will not have difficulties for replenishing the stock. However, if you sell close-outs or one-time buys, you might experience difficulties when it comes to replenishing your stock.

3. Focusing just on one product or diversifying. There are plenty of tools you can use on Amazon to let you know how well your products are performing. If you choose to sell just one product on Amazon, you can use alerts and forecasting tool available on this platform. You can also try to use tools like the ones provided by www.forecastly.com.

4. Knowing how to discover old inventory and how to deal with it. Not all the products are very popular like your best sellers, so these products may end up being stored in Amazon's warehouses for an extended period. It's highly recommended you sell these goods on other channels to avoid higher storage fees. FBA allows you to track your old inventory very easily, while the FBM options are not very helpful, forcing the merchant to search the inventory by SKU and find products manually.

5. Understanding every cost. Most of the merchants selling on this platform have a basic understanding of expenses related to the SKU level profitability, but this can only lead to an overall result that doesn't provide you too much valuable information. A better approach should be to find out the best SKU, the one that provides the highest profits, and the products that are not bringing any money. When the merchant has a detailed situation regarding the costs, it can help them understand a lot better the overhead expenses and acknowledge that these costs can be integrated into the total amount.

6. Finding out who sells the exact product on Amazon. You don't have to do a comprehensive research study on this platform to find out if somebody else is selling the exact product. There might be several merchants selling the same goods, and they might think of offering the best price, so to compete against one another, they drop the price until it becomes too low in order to be sustained (it's no longer covering the basic costs). As expected, profits are very low, or the merchants might even experience losses.

As a piece of advice, you have to check the products that you are planning to sell if they are sold by other merchants and at what prices. You need to do this before creating your account. There's really no point of selling a product on Amazon that is already sold massively on this platform, possibly even by this retailer. It's highly important to conduct this study to understand if you have a chance of making some profits in this market niche. Such a category is definitely not recommended if you want to make some profit.

***

Keep in mind that Amazon charges you only after the first 30 days of use, so you need to take advantage of this period and set your account properly. This is the perfect opportunity to create your own product offers and start selling in order to activate your merchandise. You will be charged after the first 30 days of using Amazon FBA, regardless of whether or not you have activity on the account or not. That's why you will need to use this chance to grow your business on this platform.

One of the best methods to increase your business on Amazon is to ask for feedback. In order to get feedback, you can use some of the "unorthodox" methods provided by websites, like feedbackgenius.com, feedbackfive.com, and salesbacker.com. These options are not quite free of charge, but you can consider getting feedback on these websites an investment worth taking. Also, such a strategy can send a powerful message to Amazon that you are oriented toward customers and you are willing to comply with the platform's performance.

Characteristics of a Good Product to Sell Online

How do you find the right product to sell on Amazon? Anyone selling on this platform has asked themselves this question. This is not an easy task. You have to consider that the product you are about to sell is already sold by another merchant, so you need to find a way to make the product profitable. What makes your product stand out? A short answer would be that the ideal product should have high demand and are not sold by many merchants (so a low competition). It's probably quite hard to find such a niche market, as it will allow you to go after your customers without having to worry about your competition. Here are the main characteristics of a good product:

1. Affordable retail price (usually between $25 and $50). It seems that the best-selling products on Amazon have prices ranging between these values. Such a price can encourage a high volume of sales and capable of covering expenses related to advertising, fulfillment, and storage. When you have plenty of sales and the price is between these values, you will end up with a handsome profit, most likely. If the price is higher than $50, chances are that the product will not have very good sales. At least theoretically, having more sales means more reviews, so your product will be more visible. That's why you need to think about the long term and try not to force huger profits.

2. *Not seasonal products.* No matter how you look at things, seasonal fluctuation should not influence the ideal income, at least not that much. You will need to consider a product that is capable of delivering profits all year round, not just during summer or winter.

3. *Fewer reviews for top sellers.* The niche you are trying to launch your product should have less than 200 reviews for the top sellers; less than 100 is even better. In this case, the fewer, the better since you don't have too much competition.

4. *Room for improvement.* You should always use the feedback received from customers to improve your product, as the version of the product you are selling is not final.

5. *Easy to manufacture.* When thinking of the product you want to sell, you will always need to consider the manufacturing part. The product should be easy to manufacture and should be made from resistant materials, so you will have to avoid the use of glass. Try to keep it simple. Don't overcomplicate yourself with electronic products, as you will need to offer technical support for it and provide an instruction manual.

Of course, you can't launch a product without doing proper research for similar products. Now that you know the tricks for choosing your products to sell on this platform. If you are still not convinced about the products you want to sell, you might want to check the list below, as it displays the most popular categories of products sold on Amazon:

- Kitchen and dining

- Pet supplies

- Sports and outdoors

- Patio, lawn, and garden

- Home and kitchen

Choosing the product(s) you want to sell on Amazon is not an easy task to do, but that's nothing compared preparing the products to be sold — and by *preparing* I don't mean picking, packing, labeling, or shipping. Preparing includes all the necessary procedures prior to selling the products on the platform.

First things first — before you do anything else related to the products you want to sell, you need to make sure you have the rights to sell them on the platform. Since there are products sold directly by Amazon and products sold by third-party resellers, regardless of the seller, buyers should rest assured that they are buying authentic products, not counterfeit ones. When it's the whole reputation of the company at risk, Amazon can't make any compromises when it comes to the quality of the products sold on this marketplace. That's why, for this company, customers come first. It's mandatory for them to monitor the quality of the products sold in this marketplace.

Amazon can only sell products from trusted sources. Unfortunately, unauthorized sellers have left their mark on this platform, and they have attracted a lot of attention lately. There are still a few sellers who try to avoid the rules, take advantage of the huge client base, or just try to diminish Amazon's outstanding reputation. If you no longer have access to your inventory but other sellers have access to it, the whole operation (yours and the marketplace) is at risk. Just think about it! You are selling a good-quality product with a fair price, and here comes along another merchant with a counterfeit product, offering a price much lower than yours.

This can seriously affect your business because you have no influence over pricing, as you don't know these merchants and you don't know whether or not they are complying with Amazon's rules or requirements. These merchants can force you to lower your price down to a level where profits are at their minimum, or you might even experience losses. In these cases, authorized merchants can't compete against these unauthorized ones. Price is often considered one of the most important factors to influence your decision when it comes to making a purchase. Customers will simply not care who sells the product as long as they get the same quality (apparently) with a price that is much lower.

How to Select Your Supplier

Nowadays, trading is done on a global scale, so there are plenty of import and export operations. You already made up your mind about the products you want to sell on this platform, but now you have something else on your mind — where to find the product that you are planning to sell.

The cost of acquisition should easily be covered through sales in order for you to get the profit that you want. Sourcing for products is not an easy task, as you can see in a few chapters of this book. When you want to sell online, you need to know what you are going up against, as the market is extremely competitive, and therefore you will need to come up with competitive prices for your products.

But how is it even possible to get competitive prices when the cost of acquisition is so high in the United States? It's really up to the merchants to source for the best products/spare parts at the best prices. Nowadays, a lot of them are turning toward China, as almost everything is manufactured in China. You will definitely find over there everything you need at incredibly low prices. This can give you the extra advantage for competitive prices, the ace up your sleeve.

After you already know your niche market and the product you want to sell, it's time to find your manufacturer or supplier on the Chinese market. Alibaba.com seems to be the right place to go in such scenarios, as this platform links Chinese manufacturers and suppliers to the rest of the world. This website makes the interaction between you and these Chinese companies a lot easier. You can easily see what they are specialized in, you can check their portfolio, and you can even find their contact details.

Every Chinese company that is present on this platform has to comply with the terms imposed by Alibaba.com, so you can expect them to be legit and you can easily communicate with them in English or in other international languages. This can encourage you to contact more manufacturers or suppliers and get every detail you need related to a bulk order (you probably want to start with 500 units). At this point, you will discuss the most important features about the product (e.g., dimensions, functionalities, unit price, shipping costs, payment terms or methods, delivery terms, and period). In order to get all this information, you don't have to fly to China and visit companies and suppliers. That would be complicated. You can find all the information by contacting these manufacturers and suppliers via Alibaba.com.

However, even when you contact these companies through Alibaba.com, you simply don't have to rush and get a bulk order immediately. The right way to go is to create a list of suppliers or manufacturers you want to work with and then order a few samples of the product you want. This is how you make sure that they understand exactly what you mean. After all, these companies will have to make the product as you want.

Communication in this phase is vital. You can receive the samples and send them your suggestions and recommendations. Don't cheap out and go for the cheapest products, as your reputation on Amazon is at risk, and low prices can automatically mean lower quality. Nobody wants to be known as the merchant who sells low-quality products. You will need to provide useful and high-quality products at a very good price. During the sampling process, it's important to focus on the delivery period (the delivery process will need to be supported by you), and you will also need to communicate with your Chinese suppliers and manufacturers for tracking your sample. You have to know that during this phase, you start your branding process on Amazon, especially if you want to sell private-labeled products on this platform. That's why you need to aim for high-quality products and you need to check the samples before ordering a massive amount of products.

The sampling phase can set the founding stone of a future collaboration between you and one Chinese company (or possibly more), so in this phase, you test the collaboration with them. The company who will deliver you the best sample (one that meets your requirements, of course) and you can communicate effectively with will be your choice as a partner on the Chinese market. These aspects should have priority before the price of the product.

Obviously, you have very clear requirements for your product. So when your sample arrives, you will need to check it and test it. In this case, the best option is to have already a few samples from different suppliers and manufacturers in front of you so you can easily tell the difference between them and decide which product to order massively. The unit price for the product you want might be a bit higher than you originally expected, but this shouldn't discourage you. You probably selected the most expensive sample even though all of them meet your requirements. Perhaps you felt like one specific product has your name on it even though it's the most expensive one. This phase is perfect for negotiations, so it's highly recommended to contact the Chinese manufacturer or supplier in order to negotiate the unit price.

Usually, these companies are open for negotiations, so you have high chances of pulling a better deal. This will get you an advantage against other merchants that sell similar products (your future competitors), so your price will be more competitive than theirs. Thus, you can expect a higher profit margin, which you can use for your benefit. You can play with it and offer discounts when you feel they can boost your sales. This phase is highly important, so you need to bring on your best negotiation skills, possibly sweeten the deal with a larger order if you are confident enough that your product will sell like hotcakes.

When you've managed to secure a deal and receive the best price for the product you want to sell on Amazon, it's time to place an order for your product. Make sure you are pleased with the product and the communication with the manufacturer. You will need to see how well your product performs on Amazon and how well it's being sold. This is why it's important to start with lower quantities and then order more if everything goes according to your plans. Bear in mind that it may take three to four weeks for your product to reach you from China, and it may take an additional one or two weeks for your products to reach the fulfillment center. You need to have all these in mind when you monitor your inventory, as you don't want to run out of stock and then wait a few weeks until you have the product again in your inventory.

At first, Amazon will not charge you using the seller account, only after 30 days, but you need to have the account fully operational from day one. When you have your first sales, you can estimate how long it will take to use all of your inventory so you can order another set of products from your Chinese partner at the right time. You can use all sorts of tools to get the data you need in order to find out which will be the highest and the lowest selling products. Hopefully, your products will have incredible success, and you will be required to order more. Larger orders can help you get a better price, so the more you turn around your inventory, the higher your profits will be. Sounds pretty exciting, right? This is the ideal scenario, but it's up to you how much you will sell.

Protecting and Controlling Your Brand on Amazon

The ideal way to sell on Amazon (and to comply with the terms, conditions, or regulations) is to have a registered trademark, but this may not be enough in order to protect your brand from unauthorized merchants. If you own a brand (with a registered trademark), you will still need some skilled legal advisors to help you defend your brand from all sorts of unlawful sellers.

Apparently, there is a gray market where regulations are vague enough, so the unauthorized merchants can take advantage of it and can still make a handsome profit of your brand. Most of these sellers know what they are doing. They have legal advisors, so they are not so easily scared with legal disputes over your brand. There is a first sale doctrine that allows unauthorized merchants to get away with it, to sell the products with your own brand without having to endure any legal consequences. So why not have a trademark that is powerful enough to overcome the first sale doctrine always mentioned by the unauthorized seller? You can find below a few of the advantages of setting a proper trademark:

1. Improve your authority over your distribution, so you don't have to send any letters to unauthorized sellers

2. Prove that there are legal consequences for the continuous sale of your products without your approval.

If you apply this trademark and include unequivocal terms, unauthorized sellers will not be able to speculate any loopholes to sell your products for their own benefit.

Unfortunately, powerful trademarks are very rare today, so not too many brands have full control over their distribution. The trademarks used by most of the brands today are not taken seriously by unauthorized merchants who can find a way to sell these products without having to suffer any legal consequences. When you are a brand owner, you are very concerned about who is allowed to sell your merchandise, but a distributor, you may only be interested in high volumes of sales, so it doesn't really matter to them who sells the products.

Amazon can also give you an extra hand with the Brand Registry program, which can help you a lot in protecting your brand on this platform. By taking this step, you are doing your best to prevent the sale of your products (at least on this platform) by an unauthorized merchant, who might even sell counterfeit products or something else entirely, causing you serious problems. Controlling the product distribution and price, having a proper trademark, and enrolling in the Brand Registry program are the best ways to protect your brand.

Now that you have this covered, you will need to move on to promoting your products. Keep in mind that the quality of your content will play an essential role in your upcoming success (or failure) on selling on this marketplace. This is why you will need to optimize your content in order for your products to be more visible. Since there are so many products listed in this marketplace, it is fair to say that it works like a search engine also. Therefore, you can advertise your products, and Google indexes them. This is why Google displays results from Amazon right on top of the results, regardless of the keywords you type in.

Extra exposure will not guarantee sales, especially if the content you have related to your product is weak. Therefore, after covering the issue with the trademarks, next, you will need to work on content for your products. How can you use the quality of your content to work for you and attract more potential buyers? This is a question that all the merchants will need to ask themselves. The secret lies with optimizing in order to be seen by more and more people. So you will need to apply the best SEO techniques to make your products more visible.

The search algorithm is definitely different on Amazon than it's on Google. Amazon uses A9, a special search algorithm designated for the marketplace. People are not just going on this marketplace to view products and their reviews; they come on it to buy. Amazon is very aware of this, and they display the most popular products first in order to significantly improve the conversion rate (views to sales). Every action and process you take in order to make the product more viewable is integrated into the SEO strategies. After all, every merchant wants to have their products displayed as high as possible when the buyer is searching for something in particular on Amazon. This is what higher rankings mean, and they can help you a lot when it comes to sales.

Can you imagine people buying products that are displayed in the last pages of the results? This is highly unlikely, as most people will just focus their attention on the first two pages of the results. Optimizing your product on Amazon is in a way very similar to optimizing it for Google (you can find more details in a different chapter of this book). However, when it comes to Amazon listings, you definitely need to consider all of the following:

- Quantity and quality of product images

- The title that best works for you

- The price of the product

After all, you can apply the latest SEO techniques to increase your product's visibility, relevance, and conversions on Amazon. You will need to find out the keywords that potential buyers mostly use and match them in your title, description, or information regarding your product. The ranking of products can be influenced a lot by many factors like text match, price, sales history, and selection. Therefore, providing complete, relevant, and optimized information about your product can seriously increase the product's visibility and sales.

However, in a highly competitive environment, SEO strategies will simply not be enough to guarantee your success. Bear in mind that for Amazon, the customer comes first, but they also want to make some money along the way. This is why they encouraged merchants to use their advertising options. Since there are around 2 million active merchants on this platform, how many do you think have already tried to sell on this marketplace but failed? Every day there are new merchants coming on Amazon and try to sell their products on this marketplace. Most of them will not succeed, as they are unable to make their products visible for a majority of buyers using this platform because of the extremely high competition. They may have very good content that is optimized, but nowadays, everyone has these things checked when they are selling on Amazon. The next level of promoting products is advertising on this platform. Amazon Advertising can be a win-win situation, as both the merchant and Amazon can benefit from it. The merchant gets the visibility they always wanted, while Amazon is making tons of money along the way. These are the advantages of advertisements:

- It helps the potential buyer to find the product they want.

- It boosts the rankings of the seller for the advertised items.

Competition is what drives most of the merchants to invest in advertising campaigns. The results are definitely worth it if your product has extremely good quality content. If you ignore this option, most likely you will find yourself outranked by sellers who are really good at the following:

- Finding the best keywords opportunities

- Bidding wisely

- Increasing their budget for advertising

- Using professionals for this service

The most popular way of advertising on Amazon is PPC advertising, and it has three main options:

- *Sponsored product ads* allow you to bid on ads for one of your products, driving traffic to your product page and significantly increasing your chances of converting views into sales.

- *Sponsored brand ads* drive traffic to your brand page, where buyers can find all your listed products.

- *Product display ads* are an option available for first-party vendors.

You can find below some tips for maximizing the results of Amazon Advertising:

1. Try to search for the keywords that are not used excessively. These keywords will come with extremely high bids. Bidding on the same keywords as others is not something recommended because you will find yourself paying too much for the bid, and this will not help you too much when it comes to profits. In this case, only Amazon will make lots of money. As a word of advice, eliminate the most expensive keywords for this method (the first ten of them). In exchange, you will need to focus on the next ones, as they are the ones you will need to bid on. You can use a lot of tools to discover the keywords you will need to use, so try to think outside the box, and do not make the same mistakes as others.

2. Don't be afraid to invest in your advertising campaign. Advertise your product, especially when you know that it can lead to higher sales and it can totally pay off for your campaign. You need to spend some money on the right keywords that can place your product in the right place and generate you handsome profits. You might find yourself in a bidding war with one of your competitors. In this case, the tools you need can give you the lead advantage. You might want to consider a tool like Bid+.

3. Choose your options wisely. You are not only limited to using the sponsored products ads; you can also try the sponsored brand ads if you have a seller account on Amazon. There isn't too much competition if you choose this option, and on top of that, you can direct customers to your brand page on Amazon store, where they will be able to see all your listed products. By doing this, you will allow the buyer to get a glimpse of all of your product, so you are making them aware of your products and brands and get higher chances of increasing your sales for all of your products. You can mix the available options to get the best of these options.

4. You can try both automatic and manual sponsored product ads. Mix both of these methods for better control over negative keywords and ad groups. As expected, manual campaigns are more targeted and a lot more efficient, but this doesn't mean that you need to rule out the automatic campaigns, as they can also deliver good results.

5. Don't just rely on the tools provided by Amazon. Go the extra mile and use as many tools as possible for even better results.

PPC stands for pay-per-click, so in this type of advertisement, you literally pay for every time someone clicks on your ad. You can get a limited number of clicks per day, so you better make sure that the content shown on your product's page is attractive enough to persuade the potential buyer not just to view the product but also to buy it. Bidding for advertising spots on this marketplace is like bidding at an auction — the merchant with the highest bid gets the spot. This is why you need to have in mind exactly how much you can afford to spend on such a campaign and the keywords you want to bid on.

You are probably not too enthusiastic about paying for Sponsored Product Ads on this marketplace, but below you can find some of the most important benefits it can offer:

a) It can introduce a new product to the marketplace. If you choose the Sponsored Product Ads option, you are basically improving the visibility of a product of your choice.

b) It can improve your sales and your rankings. More sales will automatically lead to a better ranking and organic search position.

c) It's definitely one of the best tools to lure new customers, if not the best. If you want to sell a product, advertise it — that should be money well spent. This is how customers will get to know your product and possibly even get hooked to it.

Chris Perry, an Amazon expert, thinks that this whole platform is an advertocracy, which can lead you to the conclusion that ads are extremely important in this marketplace, and organic search is slowly becoming less important. Keep in mind that 54% of the customers are starting their product search on Amazon, and 65% of them are only clicking on the products displayed on the first page (Wallace et al., 2019). And guess where most of the ads are placed? On the first pages obviously.

If you are not using this service, then you are:

- Giving away a great advantage to your competitors

- Leaving better placement spots for your competitors

- Just saving money while your competitors are getting the most out of this platform — better rankings, more sales, and more reviews

Advertising may be a significant step to get your product in the buyer's shopping cart, but it may still not be enough. The most powerful tool to convince a person to buy a product online is the product review. When the person doesn't have the product physically in front of them, having the best pictures of the product, very detailed product specs sheet, and the best advertising techniques still won't be enough to convince someone to buy a product. This is where the reviews kick in, as nothing can persuade a potential customer more than social proof. All consumers can leave behind a product review, mentioning the quality of the product, the price, how it looks, or the service they receive. In order to get plenty of positive reviews, you will have to sell loads of your product. Stick to your philosophy and offer the best quality for the best price possible. Make sure you deliver the product within the set timeframe — if possible, within 24 hours or 48 hours (if the distance is longer). Contact the customers after buying your product, thanking them for their choice, but also monitor the shipping of the product and ask for feedback after the product was received or after it's been used for a while. If you create a special bond with your customers, then you will get most likely more and more positive reviews.

When you plan to sell on Amazon, you will need to create your own account on this platform. You can get the individual or professional account, judging on the sales you are planning to have. Then you can select the fulfillment type, FBA (Fulfillment by

Amazon) or FBM (Fulfillment by Merchant). Usually, FBA comes with plenty of benefits in order to convince you that selling on this platform is worth it. After you select the option that best suits your needs, you will need to have to work on your products you want to list. This is not just physical preparation like picking, packing, labeling and so on. It also refers to the content displayed on the product page — title, content, meta description, photos, and most importantly, the use of keywords. This can help your products to be more relevant when customers are searching for specific products.

Keywords are the backbone of SEO strategies, but this platform doesn't rely just on organic search to display the products. It also relies on advertising and reviews to get higher rankings and to boost sales. This is what you have to do when you already know what you want to sell on this platform. Of course, your product listings will be influenced not only by the demand and request but also on how easy you can get the product (supplied or manufactured). There are plenty of merchants nowadays who approach the Chinese market to get the products they want to sell. Whether they approach the manufacturer directly or a supplier, getting in contact with a company in China seems to be the right way to go nowadays. However, sourcing for products or different spare parts on the Chinese market is not an easy task, so you will need to consider a lot of potential obstacles like customs taxes, overseas shipping, and many more. More details about sourcing can be found in other chapters of this book.

When launching your products on Amazon, you have to do it in style; otherwise, the huge Amazon community will not know about your products. Therefore, before you launch your products, there are still some things to be done in order to make sure your product will have success right from the beginning. There are a few things that have to be done before launching your product. Reviews are the most powerful tool when it comes to persuading a potential customer to buy a product. SEO and advertising both play a decisive role in improving your rankings to make your product more visible. Most of the Amazon users don't bother to search on the third or fourth page of results, so the real challenge is to get your products on the first two pages. This is where SEO and advertising can help. They can both increase the product visibility, but when it comes to converting views into sales, nothing is more important than reviews, as they are the social proof that your product has quality, does what it is supposed to, or is delivered in a timely manner. That's right! Reviews can cover topics like the product's quality, function, appearance, and delivery. Of course, the images and product description (you can have a very catchy product description, written like a story) are important, but when you have several users praising your product, then these reviews will determine other users to buy your product. You do know that a picture can say a thousand words, but it still won't matter more than the opinions of other people related to your product.

So why not have a pre-launch of your product? Send your product to some users for free in exchange for their honest opinion. Ask them to rate the user experience, quality of the product, and shipping. Your product is now in beta phase, so when you ask them for an opinion, you can use the feedback to make some tweaks to your product in order to satisfy the customers' needs. If you do want to use this feedback as constructive criticism, then you have to be very serious about this task. Some merchants like to pay a lot of people in exchange for positive reviews. This can make a huge difference at the beginning, but when reality strikes, you can have a lot lower sales than you had when you launched the product. A serious merchant would like to have a growing trend in sales. That's why they need honest opinions from users. If merchants can see feedback as constructive criticism, then they can easily transform the product to become a lot better and a lot more appreciated.

Keep in mind that false feedback will not get you far, and as soon as your product hits the market and customers are using your product, they will not hesitate to provide negative reviews. Nothing spreads faster than bad news (honestly not even wildfire), so you might want to save yourself from this unpleasant situation and make sure that your product reputation is built on honest reviews.

The practice of "artificially" increasing your ratings by paying a bunch of people to provide you positive reviews is not accepted by Amazon. After all, it's not just your reputation that is at risk but also theirs, as buyers may think that only poor-quality products are sold on this platform or the product description or images don't match the product at all. This is why Amazon has in place some very strict terms and conditions related to this practice. However, you can still find some tools you can use to get some honest reviews. Amazon really wants to protect its customers from poor-quality products. That's why they are doing everything they can to eliminate products with fake reputation. If you have poor-quality products, you might trick a customer into buying your product once (if they are under the influence of some fakes reviews), but that customer will definitely not buy from you again. Everything from the quality of the product to the product description, customer service provided (when the customers ask for more information regarding the product), and the shipping is reflected in your review. So you better excel at all these aspects in order to win your customer's loyalty. A satisfied customer will most likely buy again from you, if not the same product, then other products.

Reviews can increase your chances of converting views into sales, but they are useless if your product doesn't hit the first pages when displaying the search results. When you are a newbie on Amazon, the users of this platform don't have any idea of your products or of your brand, so becoming visible is perhaps your biggest challenge. When you have the best SEO techniques applied, this can increase your rankings a bit, but is it enough to be shown in the first pages? Most of the merchants (at least the serious ones) have their content fully optimized, so let's face it, "pure" SEO will not be enough. What you need is a lot more than that. You might want to invest in a PPC campaign to bid on the keywords you think are most likely to be typed in.

Running a sponsored products ads campaign is exactly what you need to launch your products in style. Your products have to be promoted properly, so the product ads campaign will allow you to reach an audience that you don't know at all. Your product will be shown on the first pages of the product search, being visible to plenty of users out there. There is no better way to make your product more visible than sponsored product ads on Amazon. However, when you launch your product, make sure you tease the launch of your product, just like movie studios are teasing their movies. If you already have a built network, use it! Make sure that everyone you know is aware that you are about to launch your products on Amazon. Send out emails and social media posts, informing your family, friends, and partners about your launch. Kindly ask them to share so that more people will know the good news that your product is about to launch. Do not just use every possible mean you have at your disposal to promote your product —

abuse it! Spread the word around and ask everyone you know to do the same thing.

Usually, when a product is launched, it's sold with a promotional price (limited offer). You can offer a discount to your first buyers, and you can try your best to make this their best shopping experience. If you are able to do all of these, then you have a bright future on Amazon. The strategy of discounts for your first products sold on Amazon (let's say 10%– 50%, depending on how much you can afford) will create the urgency effect among buyers, so they will rush to buy your product if they find it interesting enough.

A very good strategy to sell on Amazon is the coupon policy. You can provide discount coupons to people in your network, so you can seriously increase your chances of getting more sales. Marketing will play an essential role during this phase, as your brand is not known by too many people and your products don't have a solid reputation to be sold that easily. Reputation and brand awareness are built in time, so you will need to be patient and look for different ways to grow your brand systematically and make your products more popular.

Assuming that you already have your content properly optimized (not to mention its high quality), giving coupons and discounts will make your product irresistible to Amazon users. After all, how many times have you heard of someone buying a product just because it was on sale (with a discount)?

Discounts will make buyers lose their minds and forget about their needs, so they buy products even though they do not need them. People think they might need the product in the future, so it's good to have it.

Marketing is all about promoting your product and encouraging the customer to buy it. When selling on Amazon, you better give your potential buyers an offer they can't refuse; otherwise, you won't succeed in this marketplace. It's really up to you what methods you use to make your product more visible and to encourage more sales. I would recommend that you use any possible method you can think of — SEO, sponsored product ads, social media posts and shares, emails to everybody you know, discounts, and Amazon coupons. Get the most out of all these sources. You never know where you can stumble on your next customer. It can be a stranger from the Amazon platform, it can somebody you don't know who noticed your post on social media, or it can be someone who received an email from you.

Amazon may be an advertocracy, but nothing matters more on this platform (just like any other online store) than reviews. When you are about to launch your product, obviously you don't have too many reviews — probably no reviews at all. The only reviews you can hope for are the ones from your pre-launch phase. The ones from your product probably need some minor adjustments. These are the honest reviews you ask for when you send the product to people that you know. These reviews should be enough to get you started; however, you don't have to stop at these ones, as you need more and more reviews.

Amazon cares for its customers, so this company will promote the products with the most positive reviews. The search algorithm used by this platform takes into consideration the number of reviews and the type (positive or negative) when calculating the rankings of the product. Getting reviews is probably the most important aspect you need to care about on this platform. Every sale can generate a review, but there are plenty of customers who won't bother to provide feedback after purchasing a product, so you may need to be persistent.

Ideally, you would like to get feedback for every sale so that each sale will generate more sales. However, in the real world, you sometimes need to follow up with the customer to get feedback. In the old days of trading, a merchant reputation was spread around through word of mouth. Reviews are the modern-day word of mouth, so things haven't changed that much, only the way how word of mouth is spread around.

When you search for a product online, what do you look for? Do you consider just the pictures and description? Is the price "blinding" you? Or do you consider the reviews on top of them all? All these aspects are extremely important, but a buyer should consider the reviews before purchasing a product.

Your potential customers rely on the opinion of other customers when checking the product. The way you interact with your customers can also score you some extra points. Your customers will rate not only the appearance of the product and its quality but also the customer support service they received. Your communication with your customers is essential, as it can make all the difference in the world. This starts with your first interaction with your customer. It can be when they ask for information regarding your product or when you confirm their order directly. It can continue when they contact you about delivery (hopefully not) if your product has not arrived yet. At this point, you will need to reassure them that they will receive their product so they don't need to worry about this aspect. When they leave their review, you can reply, thanking them for buying from you and for sharing their opinion.

In order to get the most out of this platform, you will need to follow the instructions below:

1. *Brainstorm your product ideas.* You can never know where you can find the best ideas for your products, you can find them on Amazon or on other platforms like eBay. You can never ignore or underestimate a potential source for finding the right ideas that you are looking for. Therefore, you will need to conduct market research on all these stores in order to find out the products or items that have instant success. By using this method, you will simply discover if the product is worth selling online, at least by you. Remember to check the "Hot New Releases" section on Amazon. Perhaps you can get inspiration from there.

2. Bear in mind the attributes of your product. Try to think of the product requirements that can turn your product into a bestseller. Without any doubt, the ideal ones should be the following:

- *Small and lightweight.* Your product should easily fit into a small box and should not be heavier than one or two pounds. By complying with these requirements, you will not be charged extra by the carrier when it ships the product from the manufacturer to you or from you to the Amazon Fulfillment Center.

- *Non-seasonal.* The changing of seasons should not influence the volume of your sales. So try not to sell Christmas decorations or Valentine's Day gift cards.

- *Unchecked.* You are probably thinking of importing products from China, so you better think of importing those kinds that don't require and additional paperwork. Some items, like toys, have a special regime and require additional paperwork, making this import very complicated. Therefore, keep it simple and try to sell products that can be easily manufactured or distributed.

- *Effortless.* The after-sales process is very important, as you might need to provide additional customer support service, the part which is not offered by Amazon. So you will need to forget about selling electronic products on this platform.

3. Conduct market research. Take the most popular products and conduct market research to check if they are worth selling or not. You can use different apps and extensions that are very good for market research. Check for possible competitors selling the same product just to see if you stand any chance against them.

4. Find all you need to know about suppliers and manufacturers. There are plenty of specialists that recommend Alibaba, so you should try to see if you can find your suppliers and manufacturers on this platform.

a) You need first to register on this website with a buyer account.

b) Try another market research on the Alibaba platform, searching for the product you are interested in.

c) Find the listings that you want.

d) Contact the product supplier and manufacturer for more details about the product, and find out how much it will cost to manufacture the quantity you require and the shipping cost. Additionally, get the information you need about customizable options, terms and conditions, payment terms, and methods.

5. Work on your packaging, logo, and design. If you lack the skills of creating an appealing logo, beautiful design, and packaging, you might need to hire a freelancer to do this work for you. You are creating a brand, so all these aspects are very important to you.

6. Select the fulfillment method. You need to consider first the volume of sales you are anticipating before choosing FBM (Fulfillment by Merchant) or FBA (Fulfillment by Amazon). If you are expecting a higher volume of sales, then the right option for you is Amazon FBA.

7. Contract a manufacturer or supplier. You will need to get a sample first from all the suppliers or manufacturers you want to work with, and the sample will have to meet your requirements. Check for its quality, appearance, and decide which company you should choose to work with. Don't let the price decide by itself. You will need to consider the quality and the communication you had with the Chinese company as well. If you can negotiate to lower the price for a product that you like the most, then you should definitely choose that company. In the final negotiations phase, you will need to discuss and agree on all sorts of different terms and conditions, including manufacture time, how long it will take for the products to reach you, and the payment terms and methods accepted.

8. Create your product listings on Amazon. This is the next phase when you already have a signed contract with a manufacturer or supplier. Please consider how long it will take for the products to be manufactured, delivered to you, and how much it will take to prepare the products and send them to the fulfillment center. This whole process can take between four and six weeks, and this is more than enough time to prepare your listings on Amazon. Make sure that the photos you use have the best quality and the content on your page is well-structured, have informative title and description, and packed with keywords. Hopefully, keywords are used in a natural manner, so the potential customer should read the description as a fluent text that makes sense. All of these aspects should make your product a lot more appealing for the customers. A private label can also help you a lot in this case.

9. Optimize, optimize, optimize. You will need to use the best SEO techniques to optimize your content, but that will probably not be enough to make your products more visible. Sponsored product ads might do the trick for you and boost your rankings, so your product is displayed on the first or second page of the search results. This type of advertising requires you to bid on the keywords you think are more likely to be typed in. So when those keywords are entered by the potential buyers, guess what products will be displayed on the first page? It's the advertised ones. You will see your product in there. If you want to discover the most popular and relevant keywords, you might need to use some specialized tools, but the end result makes these tools definitely worth trying.

Price is important when selling on this platform, so you will need to check the average price for the product you want to sell. If the average price is $25, then you shouldn't sell lower than $20 or higher than $30.

All of these aspects will make your product more appealing, but if you do want to turn views into sales, you will need to have positive reviews. More sales should mean more reviews and the other way around. You have to use every possible opportunity to get a review from a customer. If it doesn't give you the feedback straight away, you may need to follow up and check how your product is behaving. Even when you launch a product, you can find a way to get honest reviews by sending the product for testing to various people, asking them for an honest review in return. This should give you an important advantage as the reviews are very influential when it comes to establishing the rankings of the products. Since Amazon puts its customers first, products with more positive reviews will be placed first. Therefore, this retailer is preventing the hassle of browsing intensively for the products with more reviews.

Chapter 18: Shopify

Some of the merchants don't have Amazon as a sales channel or as a primary sales channel. They prefer simply to rely on their own website when it comes to selling to customers. If you do want to sell on your own website, you need to be aware of what you are exposing yourself to. You will be responsible for everything from sourcing to storing, packing, labeling, and shipping of the product. You are also responsible for the sales channel, as you need to make sure it's appealing, responsive, and user-friendly so the customers feel attracted to it and want to use this channel furthermore. There are several things you need to implement to your own webshop, but Shopify can give you a hand with all of these, as it's an e-commerce platform designed to help you start, grow, and manage your business. Here are its uses:

- It can develop and customize your webshop.

- It allows you to sell on multiple sales channels, like physical locations, online marketplaces, mobile platforms, pop-up shops, and social media.

- It can manage your products and inventory and handle payments and shipping.

Merchants are using all kinds of templates or systems to build their very own online shop. Usually, this process requires developing or web design skills, so sellers may need to hire a specialized company to get their webshop built. If you don't want to complicate yourself with the use of latest technologies, programming languages, and frameworks, there is a solution for you. Shopify is a cloud-based platform that can be used with your webshop (integrated), so you don't have to worry too much about maintaining your webshop, software, and web servers, as well as getting the latest upgrades for the technology you are using for your website. Therefore, you will need a device to access your webshop and an internet connection to access your webshop anytime, anywhere.

There is a trial version for Shopify, which consists of a period of days. During this period, you should be able to use the service absolutely free without having to register or provide any card details. When you are creating your very own website or online shop, web developers will ask you for a one-time fee, so you may use it without having to worry about any other expense (perhaps just hosting fees). The amount may be high enough that some merchants quit the dream of having their very own webshop. If you don't want to pay for a service upfront, not before having a clear idea of how well a website performs, perhaps you want to pay just a monthly fee of your profits. Shopify understands you perfectly. That's why it offers you the option to pay a monthly subscription to use this service.

The price for the basic package is $29 per month, and with this package, you can develop your online store (including blog and e-commerce website), you have an unlimited number of products that can be sold, and you have various sales channels (according to the country you are activating) and two staff accounts. Moreover, you have the option to create manual orders and SSL certificates (security measures, discount codes), as well as the option to recover an abandoned cart. But that's not all, as you can benefit from a shipping discount of up to 64%. You can print your own shipping labels, and you can also take advantage of the fraud analysis.

There is a fee involved for paying online with credit cards, a fee that consists of 2.9% + 30 cents, and another fee for paying in-person (in this case, the fee is just 2.7% if the payments are made using a credit card). Also, there is a 2% additional fee if the payment is made by other payment providers than Shopify payments.

The basic package can support three different types of points of sale — the Shopify POS app, third-party POS apps, and of course, the hardware peripheral support. There are still some extra fees in there, but overall, the package sounds interesting enough, especially because it includes the basics for starting a new business of online selling.

However, the basic Shopify package may not be satisfactory enough for merchants who want to sell more. This is why some sellers choose the standard package, which includes all the features that are in the basic package, plus a lot more. The package costs $79 per month, but it has gift cards and professional reports for you. You will have five staff accounts and shipping discounts of up to 72%. You also have the option to print out your shipping labels, as well as the option for USPS Priority Mail Cubic pricing and fraud analysis.

Payments are charged a bit less than the basic package. For credit card payments made online, you will get charged 2.6% + 30 cents. On the other hand, the in-person credit card rate is just 2.5% + 0 cents. If merchants are using a different payment provider than Shopify payments, the fee is just 1%. When it comes to the points of sale, this package will support Shopify POS app, third-party POS apps, register shifts, and hardware peripheral support. There are also unlimited Shopify POS staff PINs. This package obviously includes more than you need for a growing business.

If you are still not satisfied with the features of the previous two packages, then you will need to take a look at the most comprehensive package that Shopify can offer. It will cost $299 per month, and it's called the advanced Shopify package. This option can support up to 15 staff accounts, advanced report builder, and very interesting shipping rates and discounts of up to 74%. Features like printing your own shipping labels and USPS Priority Mail Cubic prices are already included.

Payments have also become more attractive, as the fee for paying online using a credit card is just 2.4% + 30 cents, while for the in-person payment with a credit card, it is just 2.4%. If you use a payment provider other than Shopify payments, then you will have to pay an additional fee of just 0.5%. When it comes to the points of sale, there is no difference between the advanced Shopify package and the standard package.

Shopify has plenty of benefits and advantages, but one of the biggest advantages is that you can use your very own domain name with this platform. In order to do so, you only have to go in the admin section of the platform and then transfer your domain over to Shopify. Therefore, you are allowing Shopify to take over your webshop and domain so that you only need to make the necessary tweaks to your domain settings, pay the fee for your domain, and renew it from the admin section of your Shopify account.

The next stage is to connect your webshop with Shopify, as the platform will display your domain name on the Shopify store. If you don't have any online store yet, then you can buy a domain from a third-party provider or directly through Shopify.

Another huge advantage is that this platform will not need you to hire any web designer or developer in order to create your very own Shopify online store. The platform has an online store builder function that will make you choose from a wide variety of themes available to create the customized webshop that you want. Also, there are some apps that can prove to be very handy and can add extra features or functionality to your store. Shopify can easily be considered one of the easiest ways (if not the easiest) to build your very own top-of-the-notch webshop, having all the features that your business needs. All of these can be achieved without hiring professional services (web building, SEO search), as Shopify can provide everything that's best for you. You will only need to select your subscription plan and add your products to this platform. If you don't have any product to sell or you don't have any place to store them, you might need to consider dropshipping as an option.

Time is often considered an issue nowadays, as people don't have that much time to spend on shopping. This is why shopping malls are becoming less and less crowded. If you want to survive as a merchant nowadays, you will need to focus more on selling online. Amazon provides possibly the best online marketplace on the planet, but you can also sell through your own online store. Perhaps you can even have better prices than the ones your set on Amazon. This is a bit unlikely. The Amazon platform is way too competitive in order to keep the prices too high, so you might want to adjust them according to the prices on the platform.

Focusing your business online will enhance the functionality of your online store in order to be more appealing and user-friendly for your customers. If you build your own client base, chances are that they will buy your product again directly from your own website. When it comes to e-commerce solutions, you can choose from plenty of tools out there, like Magento, OpenCart, PrestaShop, BigCommerce, or WooCommerce. Shopify has managed to outrank all of these tools, and it is probably the most popular e-commerce tool as it can provide the following:

1. *An easy-to-set-up and user-friendly platform.* Shopify can help your webshop to become one of the most successful ones on the web, and the best part is that it's so easy to install and to use. Forget about website development, hosting your webshop, or other things related to technical features. Shopify can build your online store from scratch with all the functionalities you need. You only need to add your name on it.

2. *Stylish webshop.* Not only is the platform is easy to use, but it can also make your webshop to look great. The platform includes great-looking templates that will definitely encourage you to develop an amazing and nice-looking online store. You can still improve it if you require a better UI and UX, so at this point, you can hire some professionals to help you with your webshop.

3. App integration. Shopify can easily integrate all sorts of apps, allowing you to properly customize your online store and integrate swiftly some apps that will allow the buyer to add the extra features or functionalities that your customer may want.

4. Security and reliability. When dealing with online transactions, website security and reliability is extremely important. After all, the website will be dealing with very sensitive data, such as card or bank details and personal details. You don't want these details to fall into the wrong hands. That's why Shopify uses powerful encryption to prevent this from happening, and it keeps pace with the latest technologies when it comes to data security, encryption, and reliability.

5. Very fast loading speed. Have you ever experienced slow loading pages when buying online? You probably encountered this issue during Black Friday or for other periods when massive sales are happening. Under normal circumstances, these issues should not be happening, but there are still plenty of cases when they actually happened. With Shopify, you don't have to worry about this issue, at least when you are experiencing a normal period of sales. The platform will guarantee that your website will load the page the customer desires in a matter of seconds.

6. Very powerful marketing tools. Shopify would not be so successful if it wouldn't take care of the marketing side. Regardless of the package you select, your online store will be properly optimized, as even the basic package has impressive SEO features and advanced analytics to measure its performance. A superior package will include other marketing tools like discount coupons, store statistics, email marketing, and custom gift cards, all features specially designed to help you boost your sales and make handsome revenue from your sales.

7. *Mobile compatible.* Keep in mind that technology is quickly becoming very advanced, and there is a lot of emphasis on mobile devices. People are not using these devices just to make calls or to stay on the internet; they are also using them to play online and to make purchases. If you ask an IT specialist, today's motto should be "Always be connected." People are always on the move, but this doesn't mean that they can't be connected to the internet. Whether they are using their tablets or smartphones, customers now have the option to view the products at high quality, check the product description and spec sheet, and hit the "Add to cart" button. Shopify always keeps up with the latest technologies and optimizes online stores to be mobile compatible as well. So if you are using Shopify, you can expect an order from someone who is on the move, on public transportation, or enjoying their coffee in a coffee shop. Its templates can be used to build online stores available on all sorts of tablets and phones. So don't worry if you are using Android or iOS — your device will be compatible with Shopify.

8. Outstanding customer support service.
When you are a global company, you simply can't ignore the importance of customer service, as it can make customers loyal. Nothing should be more important to a huge company than customers, so providing support to them should have the highest priority. Shopify understands perfectly the value of its customers. That's why it provides different options for support like 24/7 phone, live chat, or email. Any issues or queries are resolved in the fastest way possible in order to prevent any inconvenience from escalating.

When you provide such benefits, it's really hard not to be one of the leaders for e-commerce tools. Headquartered in Canada and with over 15 years of activity (the platform was launched in 2004), Spotify has slowly worked its way to the top to become probably the most powerful and popular e-commerce tools you can find online.

Chapter 19: Optimizing Your Own Webshop Using the Best SEO Techniques

Search engines have to deal with more and more websites every day as the number of existent websites is getting closer to 2 billion. Fortunately, only a few hundreds of millions of websites (still too many of them, I know) are active at the moment. Imagine if all of them are displayed by a search engine! Just picture the chaos in this case! There are a few rules that can be applicable in this case in order to arrange and rank websites. These sets of rules and regulations are all gathered in the search engine optimization, as all the changes you make can maximize your rankings and make your website more visible for the wide audience. There are some important elements that can have a serious impact on your rankings, such as the following:

- Entry and exit pages

- Titles

- Site content

- Graphics

- Website structure

However, there are still some other factors you will need to consider that can have a serious impact on rankings. Don't forget about keywords, links, meta description, and HTML. If you want your website to perform and have higher rankings, you will need to use SEO techniques. However, you can have your website optimized but still have pretty low rankings. When SEO is not enough, some people use "unorthodox" methods like update frequencies and advertising campaigns. You will need to understand that SEO doesn't rely just on one process; it represents a compilation of strategies and procedures specially designed to improve the rankings of your website — or in other words, to increase the website's visibility. If you expect this to be a once-in-a-lifetime process, think again! Technologies are evolving. People are trying more and more different things in order to increase the rankings, so you will need to optimize your website constantly to get better rankings.

This is why SEO is ongoing, and it should never end. You will always have to be one step ahead (at least) of your competition. Bear in mind that people find your website when they type in the search query some keywords. You have to be proactive and anticipate the keywords that users type in so that your website comes among the first results.

Another aspect that is crucial to rankings is localization. Your search engine (most likely Google) will show matching results first, but it will also take into consideration the relevance. For example, it will not show sellers of pet food from a few hundred miles away. You can consider SEO as a technique of manipulating the search engine to work for your own benefit. You will need to consider the following details when implementing any SEO strategies or methods:

- Use meta tags, high-quality content and graphics, and relevant keywords. All of these combined can improve your rankings.

- Make sure the keywords are used naturally so they don't appear forced in the context.

- Usually, having some relevant and legitimate links on the website is highly recommended.

- SEO will not be enough nowadays, especially if you want your website to perform. If you have an online store, you need to use some interesting marketing campaigns and keyword advertising. As an example, Amazon uses PPC advertising to allow merchants to bid on specific bids. This will place the products on the first page, determining the potential customers to click on the product and therefore increasing the chances of converting the view into a sale.

You can't begin to optimize your website without having a clear plan set. Such a plan will need to include the goals you want to achieve, your strategies and how to implement them, and a way to measure and monitor your results and performances. Nothing is final — goals or strategies can change over time, according to the results you are getting. It's really hard to think of an even more dynamic field, and SEO is changing extremely fast. What is working today may not work tomorrow. This is why you always need to have a flexible approach when it comes to SEO and keep an open mind for the latest technologies and techniques from this field.

Search engines will always value SEO, unlike some marketplaces where ads are becoming far more important than SEO. The purest strategies for optimization are all included in organic search techniques. Have you ever wondered what criteria Google or other search engines use when displaying the websites? The criteria are shown below:

- Content

- Site maturity

- The website's language

- Topical links

- Title tags

- Keywords

- Link context

- Anchor text

- Site popularity

Search engines have their very own algorithms to calculate the rankings of a website. If you understand what criteria are considered the most important for the search engine, you can work on optimizing it and significantly improve your chances to boost your rankings. Without dedicating your time to optimize your content, you are leaving the rankings of your website to chance. Well, guess what? Some of your competitors are a lot more determined and may be doing some serious optimizing at this very moment. Chances are that their website will outrank yours. Your SEO plan will need to include some steps:

1. *Prioritize your pages.* Most likely, your website will contain more pages, so it's highly important to structure your website properly and steer traffic to the pages that the wide audience might be interested in. If you manage to do this task well, you can find yourself with an increased income (don't expect miracles, though, as SEO will not boost your sales by 500%).

2. *Assess your website.* Try to evaluate your website in the most objective manner! Discover its weak points and work on them to improve and optimize them. The elements of the website can be seen below:

- *Meta tags.* Meta description can attract people to a certain page as it's something that pops into the eyes of the user when the website is displayed in the search engine. The title also plays an essential role in this case, as it can also be seen on the pages of the search engine. The title and meta description will need to be very appealing; otherwise, they will not get too many users to your website.

- *Content.* Keeping your content updated is highly important, as users are not interested in outdated content. In order to get the users interested, you will need to have fresh content.

- *Links on the site.* Understanding how a search engine works is crucial. You need to know that it has some "crawlers" used to track down data, retrieve it, and display it. Well, these "crawlers" are capable of tracking even the links you have on your page, and such aspect can have a positive impact on your rankings. However, you will need to make sure that these links are functional; otherwise, it can negatively affect your rankings.

- *Site map.* This might sound a bit strange, but the site map can also influence your rankings. Search engines analyze whether the site map works or not. If the links of the site map are working properly, then this can be an extra bonus point for your rankings. If not, it can surely be problematic.

3. Finish the plan. After evaluating your website, it is highly important to focus on the areas that need improvement. Over time, these areas that require extra attention may change, and this may lead to a change of plan.

4. Monitor the results and implement new strategies. There are plenty of tools you can use to measure the performance of your SEO strategy. During this phase, you are basically testing the strategy, so if the results are far from being satisfactory, then you need to take immediate actions to change the strategy. If everything is on track, then this may be the perfect opportunity to have some clear results.

***

As mentioned, the SEO plan should include a set of goals you are trying to achieve for your website and some strategies that you will need to implement in order to achieve those goals. You need to focus your goals on visibility, website traffic, and the return on investment, but let's take them one at a time.

Visibility can be considered, in this case, a synonym to branding. SEO is looking to get better rankings, so the product will be displayed higher in the search results. Better rankings can also mean increased visibility, as users can see the link to your website right before their eyes, read the title and meta description, access the site, find out what the website is about, and become aware of it. Marketing specialists would call this process "brand awareness." Even if this doesn't apply all the time, high rankings can be associated with brand endorsement. When some keywords include brand terms, the search engine can display results that can also include your brand. Nothing is perfect, but a very good strategy should aim for perfection and try to boost the rankings of your website to make it more visible if the SEO strategy is focused on branding or visibility.

Steering more traffic to their website is what many people are interested in, so having higher traffic to the website is one of the main goals of SEO. You might be able to develop a superior website, with high-quality content, but this is simply not enough to get more traffic to your website. However, the techniques you used to optimize the website yesterday may already be obsolete today, so you always have to adapt to the latest trends.

There are way too many websites nowadays, and there is increased competition. You may have several websites displaying similar content to yours;

therefore, you might be facing a more serious competition than you initially thought. How can you get more traffic to your website? SEO can give you a hand, as a proper strategy can steer traffic to your website, traffic that might convert into sales. It can play the role of a skilled salesman, as it brings prospects to your website from a crowd of people that probably never heard of your website and most likely were not even interested in your website at all.

Keep in mind that keywords can help you rank higher in the results displayed by the search engine. When a potential customer types something into the search engine, you will need to anticipate the keywords entered. You can conduct a study to find out the most used keywords that are most relevant to you. If the ones entered in the search query matches yours, then you will most likely get significantly more traffic.

One of the main goals of SEO can be a higher return on investment. If the first two goals are already achieved, some people aspire for something higher. This can be the case of companies that might be looking to increase their sales and get more leads or more advertising revenue. Some other organizations may not focus that much on monetizing their website. They might focus on promoting or sharing a particular message or getting more people to sign up for a newsletter.

An SEO strategy can concentrate its actions to achieve one of the goals mentioned above. Obviously, a higher return on investment for companies can mean paying for SEO (probably even for advertising) and getting their money back through sales. More views can lead to more sales in most of the cases, so it's highly effective to spend money to promote your website, have it properly optimized, and have the right content that can easily persuade users to become buyers on your website.

There is no SEO strategy to fit all companies out there, so according to the business that you are having or the website that you are running, there may be different needs or goals. SEO is all about customization, finding the tailored solution to increase your rankings, so when you are trying to come up with such a strategy, you may need to answer the next questions:

- What exactly are your promoting (information, product, service)?

- What is your target market (target audience)?

- What about your brand?

- What kind of website content are you planning to use on this website (images, videos, articles, case studies, and so on)?

- Is your website structure and content easy to modify?

- How well do you know your competition?

- Can you focus on developing your content?

- What resources can you use and what are the release dates?

Understanding the traffic on your website and the visitor's intent should start with query types. They can be split into different categories:

1. Navigational query. This has the intention of steering traffic to a specific page or website. For example, a person can type into the search query the company domain name. If they want to go to a specific site, they can type in "Facebook," for instance.

2. Informational query. This is intended to get an answer to a question (broad or direct) or to find information about a specific topic without having a source in mind. You can type in the search query "yoga poses," for instance.

3. Transactional query. This is the kind of specific search that can lead to a sale. Just imagine that someone is typing a certain model of TV or digital camera. This can only make you believe that the person is interested in buying, so first, they try to get more information about the product specifications and find the best prices out there to compare. If you want to apply for a loan or even a mortgage, you will type in the search query "personal loan" or something else, and you browse through the results. To compare the interest rates or other fees, you might want to open the pages in separate tabs.

***

There are a few business factors that you will need to consider when developing an SEO strategy. These factors can be seen below:

- *Business models and revenues.* In this case, you will need to think about the purpose of the site and its ability to generate revenue — basically how much money your website can make. This is where the purpose of the website is very important, as it can be created for selling products or services, advertising, generating leads, or getting more subscribers or members. Regardless of the purpose, all of them should be considered methods to monetize the website.

- *Targeted customers.* Every time you are releasing something, like a product, you have in mind your target audience or customers. This is applicable to websites as well, as it can be dedicated to a specific age group, people living in an area, or people of a specific gender.

- *Competitors.* Chances are that you are not the only one seeing an opportunity on the market, so you will not be the only one with a website dedicated to a specific topic. Most likely, you will have competition as well, so acknowledging your competitors should not be missing from any SEO strategy. You will need to have some basic marketing knowledge in order to figure out your market share and your position on the market in order to set your goals accordingly.

- *Branding goals.* Such a factor can only refer to the visibility of your website when somebody types in the search query the name of a brand.

- *Content development.* Whether your website will have success or not highly depends on the content that you are using. If you have quality content that is also optimized, your website will most likely have more traffic, and the purpose of the website should be easily achieved. When it comes to optimizing the content of your website, most of the techniques are focused on the use of keywords, title and meta description, social media sharing, and external and relevant links.

- *Search habits of people.* Understanding how people search for products that are similar to yours is very important, but it requires complex research to find the search queries that customers normally use in the search engine.

***

SEO is all about understanding your audience (in this case it refers to the people visiting your website) and their search habits, as well as focusing on the right niche in order to develop your business. A targeted audience will have a serious impact on the website design and will set your content management and SEO strategies. The factors mentioned above may not be enough to come up with a proper SEO strategy, so you will need to have more things to consider.

1. *Map your products and services.* Such a consideration can only refer to understanding how your business works, or to be more specific, what information, products, or services can you provide for your audience or potential customers. This is how you can gather more information about your customers, like location, age group, gender, and so on so that you will know for sure what audience you will need to target in the future.

2. *Make sure your content has extremely high quality.* It's very important to get more traffic to your website. Having stuff that is already showing up on other websites will not do you any good, so you will need to focus on creating original and high-quality content. Keywords and website structure are also included in your content, and by now, you already know how important they are for generating traffic to your website. After all, "the crawlers" of a search engine are going through all your content, and they can help the search engines understand what your website is about and how relevant it is to the search query typed in by people who are searching for different things over the internet. In order to remain in business, you will need to have relevant content; otherwise, your website will not be displayed when someone types in a query search. On top of that, your content is also highly important for link development and content marketing, as they are both affected by it.

3. *Categorize the audience of your site.* Without any doubt, one of the most important things you need to do when you are creating your very own SEO strategy is to conduct market research to discover the keywords that can drive traffic to your website. Compiling a list with all these keywords and knowing how frequent they are used in the search queries will make you understand the targeted audience.

4. *Understand your competition in the market you are operating.* When trying to implement an SEO strategy, you should always consider your competition. What are they doing and how you can outrank them? Be ahead of everyone. An organic search may not be enough in many cases, as people are becoming more and more aware of the rankings when it comes to the displayed results in the search query. Of course, the ideal situation is to get more sales with minimum costs, but you may still need to invest in advertising, as perhaps your competition is already doing that. When it comes to

SEO, investing in keyword advertising can be considered normal, so people who want to promote their website may want to invest in a PPC (pay-per-click) campaign. In this case, the website owner will pay a cost for every click people are making to access their website. This method has the purpose of generating more traffic to the website.

In order to get more info about keyword competitiveness, you might want to consider using a tool like Google AdWords Keyword Planner. This will enable you to check the cost-per-click of a campaign if you bid on a target phrase. When you have higher prices for this campaign, this can only mean that these terms are extremely competitive in an organic search. In such cases, you will need to focus on studying your competitor. Try to understand what they are doing and adapt your SEO strategy according to it. You might be facing different sorts of scenarios, such as the following:

- Your competitor is using unique and highly converting keywords (capable of converting views into sales).

- Your competitor is using a high-value and targeted link.

- The market segment of your competitor is already saturated, and in this case, you will need to focus on a different segment.

Discover the flaws and weaknesses of your competitor's strategy and exploit them as your opportunities. An SEO strategy is very similar to a marketing one, as it involves finding out the strengths and weaknesses of your competitors and using them to your own benefit. You will need to be very careful when analyzing the link strategies of your competitor because some of them might be using some link tactics (for a short period of time), and they can get sanctioned by the search engine. If you want to discover the performance of your competitor's SEO, it's highly recommended to use tools like SearchMetrics and SEMRush.

There may be different SEO strategies for various situations, such as raw traffic, e-commerce sales, mindshare and branding, lead generation and direct marketing, reputation management, and ideological influence. The most important aspects that you will need to consider in all these situations are when to apply the strategy, what keywords you need to look for, and creating and optimizing the content.

In the first situation, when the strategy is to generate raw traffic, the strategy consists of a compilation of techniques that don't involve any paid advertising. So there isn't a specific moment when this is highly recommended, but this should be used as an introductory strategy, just to see if it reaches the goals you set. This type of SEO will encourage you to develop high-quality content and use keywords in every bit of text you have on the website (like headlines, meta description, titles, or even file names). How exactly does a well-structured website look like? It should have all kinds of categories and subcategories — this is definitely a plus, and it can help your website rank higher on the results page.

Applying an SEO strategy for e-commerce sales is highly recommended when you have an e-commerce website, like an online shop, where customers can buy products directly from your site. Keywords can lure traffic to your website, but is the organic search approach sufficient in this case? When the success of your online shop is at risk, you are willing to spend for paid advertising, PPC campaigns in which you bid on your selected keywords. The SEO strategy for e-commerce sales is all about maximizing the potential of keywords. It's very interesting to discover the ROI (return on investment) for every keyword you targeted. When you focus on specific search queries or brand-related queries, such a strategy can lead to more sales.

When it comes to your content, there is no big difference for the creation part, but for the optimizing part, there are some differences between this strategy and the previous one. To properly optimize your content, you may need to share it through social media and maximize the role of organic search. Great-quality content can encourage traffic and more sales.

When you use SEO for mindshare and branding, the key aspects can be different. You can use this strategy if your goal is not to sell but to deliver a message. When you take the money part out, keyword targeting seems to be less important, so you are not willing to spend money on advertising. You are not trying to monetize the website; you are only trying to make sure that your message is received by more and more people. However, this doesn't mean that you should completely ignore keywords. You should use them, but you can use longer keywords to make sure you get satisfactory results. In this case, nothing seems to be more important than your content from the site. Therefore, it's highly recommended to have a well-structured website with clickable structures to make navigation through this website a lot easier.

You can use also use SEO for direct marketing and lead generation, and you will have the same factors to look for. This strategy may be applicable when you operate a website on which you sell your products or services, but users will have to inquire about possible offers. Longer keywords can have better results in this case because the customers reaching to you may not have a very clear idea of what they want, hence the enquiring part. When it comes to content and how to optimize it, in this case, the product or service is not displayed, but the website still has to contain valuable information to get the customer interested. Creating high-quality content can be a very big challenge, and the success of your website depends on it.

When it comes to implementing SEO for reputation management, these factors may have a different use or impact. You can use this type of SEO to protect your brand from some negative results or when you already eliminated negative content. The keywords can't be more specific than the ones used in this case as they have to be a brand's or a person's name. The content creation and optimization couldn't be more important as it combines the optimization of pages from plenty of various domains in order to demote negative listings. In this case, the use of social media profiles or other third-party platforms, press releases, links from networks of sites, and public relations is highly recommended with classic SEO practices.

If your website is for ideological influence, there is a special SEO technique for such a website. In this category, you can include websites for political parties that are very active during electoral campaigns. The keywords used in this case have to be related to influencing decisions or thinking, so you will need to think of ideas like *debates* and include in your query "pros" or "cons." The content displayed on such websites plays a very important role, so choose your words wisely. They have to be very convincing and inspiring. Putting links in there will definitely add an extra advantage for you.

Do you want to give your competitors a run for their money? Then according to the website you are operating, you can implement the SEO strategy that best suits your needs. However, all of them have to be measured in order to find out how well they can perform. You have the SWOT analysis (just like in marketing) but also the SMART plan (specific, measurable, achievable, realistic, and time-bound). The starting point for every research and analysis is acknowledging your place in the market. The SWOT analysis stands for strengths, weaknesses, opportunities, and threats. You will need to bear in mind that the origin of strengths and weaknesses are internal, while the opportunities and threats come from the outside.

The first step of this analysis is to identify your strengths; therefore, you will need to consider all of the following:

- What sources are generating most of your traffic to your website or business?

- Do you have any partnerships or projects that can drive a positive momentum toward getting more traffic and revenue?

- What are the sections or types from your content that are generating you most of your traffic, conversions, and ROI?

- Did you make any changes in the past in order to get a higher value (traffic, conversion, and of course, ROI)?

We have to admit it! It's a lot harder for us to admit our weaknesses, but you still have to be objective and serious enough to spot them. This is why you will need to ask yourself a few questions, such as the following:

- Do you have any traffic sources that are performing less than expected?

- What is your content type that causes you low traffic?

- What changes you applied in the past to make a significant difference didn't work?

- What partnerships or projects are not handled well?

Finding opportunities requires you to look more outside than inside, but you will still need to consider your strengths. Only if you acknowledge them will you be able to find opportunities for your website or business. Opportunities have external origins, but it also makes you look on the inside. The process of finding your opportunities will reveal to you the areas in which you are performing properly, where you can expand, and the areas you didn't explore yet. In this case, you will need to ask yourself:

- Which projects or ideas that you haven't developed and tested might have a big impact on your website or business?

- What weaknesses can be repaired?

- What sources that provide higher-quality traffic can you use to expand and to generate a higher value?

- Which changes that were used to make a difference worked? Can they be applied on a more extensive scale in order to get an increased value?

- Which markets or content areas are favorable for an expansion?

- What forms of social media can you used to get more traffic?

- Which links or new content you haven't tried yet?

Probably the hardest part of a SWOT analysis is to find threats, as you will need to mix your creative thinking with an honest evaluation of your competitor's strengths in comparison with your own weaknesses. This is how you can reach the right conclusion, but below you can find some of the most important questions you will need to ask yourself in order to identify these threats.

- If you consider the area of your weaknesses, who are the key players in the market? How they have achieved such success?

- Which changes referring to market conditions, human behavior, or internet usage can dramatically impact the market?

- Who are the key players in your field of expertise? How they achieved this success? Where exactly can they interact with your customers or your business?

As previously mentioned, SMART stands for specific, measurable, achievable, realistic, and time-bound, so let's take them one by one, to find out what they really mean.

When developing your very own SEO strategy, you need to set your *specific objectives,* as they are vital for the success of your website or business. You can't have vague objectives, as they will not lead you anywhere. Some good examples of specific objectives would be more views, more leads, or more customers.

Measurable objectives are those that can easily show how well your website is performing, as they have some numbers next to it. There are plenty of analytics software you can use to get the numbers you need to make informed decisions.

SEO should also be about setting *achievable objectives* with the existing resources you have, so your main principles to follow are feasibility and sustainability. Don't go chasing extremely high objectives, as you might find yourself spending too much money on advertising and getting less than expected in return.

Realistic objectives should be the ones you are determined to perform. You should apply the right SEO strategy that will get you more traffic and additionally convert views into sales. Aiming high is one thing, as long as you don't set utopian objectives, so make sure that the objectives that you set can be achieved using the resources you have at your disposal and with little effort.

Performance is strongly linked with a period of time, so when you set your objectives, you have to allow yourself a time frame to achieve the objectives. Setting tight deadlines or milestones can be good for your performance, as it encourages you to perform better in a shorter period of time. This is what *time-bound objectives* are all about.

Chapter 20: Using eBay for Online Sales

You simply can't talk about online platforms without mentioning eBay, one of the most popular websites where you can sell almost anything. The fun part is that this website is available for most of the people, even simple people trying to sell grandpa's watch. eBay has created new opportunities, not just for companies and shops but also for the simple folk. This platform is best known for its consumer to consumer auctions and sales. There are high chances of you finding used products on this platform, and there are also incredibly high chances of finding great deals here. You will find most of the things in here, from baseball cards, ancient coins, and rare collectibles to usual stuff you can find in a regular shop (but it's not necessarily new).

The website was launched in 1995, and since then, it has become extremely popular worldwide, becoming the global phenomenon that we know today. Nowadays, there are many merchants using this platform as a sales channel, although most likely eBay is not the primary sales channel. Still, it can generate you a very handsome additional income.

The website is available in different countries worldwide and has over 250 million users in 2017.[1]

One of the biggest advantages of eBay is that anyone can create an account with them (basic account) for free. Of course, you can go for the seller account, which will have some fees involved for listing (for example). Such fees can have different values depending on the price of the product you want to sell and on how long the product is listed.

The basic account will allow you to buy and sell products on this platform, while the seller account has a few more features. Just to understand how much the platform has evolved over the years, just think that millions of transactions are made every day on eBay. The popularity of this platform increased after the name eBay was mentioned on TV, news, movies, and through word of mouth.

This platform appears to be the number-one website for collectors, as they can find a wide variety of rare collectibles. eBay has advanced search tools, notifications, a user-friendly platform, and anti-fraud systems available (designed to prevent fraudulent transactions). The most passionate collectors can spend hours on this website, searching

---

[1] https://expandedramblings.com/index.php/ebay-stats/

for the best deals of rare collectibles, buying and selling them.

If you choose to roll with eBay, there are plenty of advantages for it. A huge variety of products can be found on this platform. It also has incredibly high traffic and awareness. Sounds interesting? Then you might want to consider the factors below if you want to sell on this platform:

1. *Traffic.* eBay is already an extremely popular platform that has huge traffic. So why not use this traffic to your own benefit? After all, this website is one of the most famous marketplaces you can find on the internet. But that's not all! To keep the traffic coming, eBay invests a lot in advertising to lure customers to their platform, so merchant could benefit from this.

2. *Fan base.* eBay may prevent you from becoming too personal with your customers, as it doesn't have the option built up for this. The communication between you and your customers is restricted on eBay. This is why eBay is mostly used by merchants as a secondary sales channel, considering that they already have their own website as the primary sales channel. eBay doesn't provide the buyer's data to the merchant, so using email addresses of your customers for future promotions is simply not possible.

3. *Costs.* This platform will not charge you a monthly subscription, so you don't have to worry about paying anything if you are not active on eBay. However, when you list products on this marketplace, you will be charged small amounts of money for each product, and you might have to pay a percentage for every sale you make on this platform. There are other costs related to the following:

- Advanced listing tools

- The use of more product categories

- The duration of the listing

All these costs can pile up and might lead you to think that a monthly subscription will be a lot more advantageous. However, you might want to do your math right. The right volumes of sales and the right amount of products listed for a short period of time will definitely bring you more profits than in the monthly subscription alternative provided by other services.

***

It all depends on your purpose, on what you want to achieve. If you are thinking of building your brand awareness and having a closer relationship with your customers, then eBay might not be the platform for you. If you don't care about your brand and just want more sales and income, then look no further as eBay is a platform for you. However, in order to be successful on this platform, you will need to consider the following tips:

1. *Prove you are trustworthy.* Naturally, new sellers have fewer sales than the experienced ones, as they are just getting to know the platform and their customers. Just like Amazon, eBay uses a feedback system that is social proof that the seller is (or not) trustworthy and the product has/ hasn't the quality customers expect. Positive feedback will build you a strong reputation, and nothing will influence more a potential customer than seeing positive reviews on the product. Selling online relies a lot on the feedback system, and eBay makes no exception. However, keep in mind that your reputation will be built over time, so don't expect to have massive sales in the first month (unless you are selling a product with extremely high demand). More sales and more reviews will improve your ratings and your credibility in the eyes of potential customers. Increasing your ratings should be your main priority, but you are probably wondering how you can do that. You can find below some of the most important tips in order to achieve this goal:

- Focus on getting more sales at the beginning. You can start by selling cheap items (preferably small). If you have a large inventory, this is how you can turn it around in a relatively short period. When you have more sales, chances are higher to get more reviews (hopefully positive ones). Try to send the product to the customer within 24 hours when possible. Fast delivery will score you some extra points for a positive review.

- Be prompt when answering your customers' queries.

- Be open when customers ask you for a refund. Don't over-argue and offer it only when you receive the product back (you need to protect yourself from potential scammers, so make sure you are not giving away things for free). Of course, there are some policies involved, so you can't offer a refund for a product purchased six months ago.

2. Make sure you have high-quality photos. When people are visiting your product page, they will need to see the clearest and top-quality photos, just to get a clear idea of what they are buying. Obviously, blurred photos will not turn views into sales, so you will need to avoid using this kind of pictures. Also, you don't want customers to get back to you saying that the photo of the product from the platform doesn't match the product they received. Make sure there are no mistakes here. You might consider yourself as really good with photos, but you still need to consider the following:

- Make sure there is proper lighting when you are taking the photos.

- Try to use a professional background.

- Try to capture as much detail as you can.

3. Research the products you want to sell.
When it comes to selling online, you simply can't rush and sell your products without knowing more about the prices of similar products or how other merchants describe their products. You will need to base your research on the following questions:

- Are the goods that you are trying to sell usually auctioned?

- Do you know how to format your description properly? How are other sellers doing this task?

- How do other merchants post their products? What angles are they using?

4. Have a well-written product description.
The product description is one of your "aces from your sleeve" to convert views into sales. It's at least as important as your photos. Keep in mind that the product description has to be catchy and original. If it is copied from somewhere else, it will seriously affect your SEO efforts. Most people would agree that copying descriptions from a product to another and then rewriting them until they are original enough, as well as catchy and persuasive, will do the trick and convert views into sales. All products descriptions use a template in order to appear more appealing to the potential customer. Make sure you stick to that

template, but customize your product description so that it best fits your needs.

5. *Become a PowerSeller*. When you sell on eBay, you simply can't aim higher than this. That's why everyone who means business and wants to grow on this platform should try to become a PowerSeller. However, this achievement requires really hard work. You need to sell on a frequent basis and provide the best customer support service out there. There are some steps you need to take in order to become a PowerSeller, like the ones mentioned below:

    a) You need to have at least 98% positive reviews.

    b) You sold more than 100 products and had more than $3,000 in sales in the previous year.

    c) You logged in on eBay for at least 90 days in a row.

Chapter 21: Highlights

Retail arbitrage is the whole process of sourcing for incredibly cheap products and selling them on different sales channels for profits. This is probably the most solid strategy to make some serious cash these days. Selling products or services is one of the most profitable business ideas, so it's no wonder that so many people choose this activity to get a constant huge revenue.

Trading is simply booming nowadays, as physical and online stores are making more money than ever before. There are many people addicted to shopping; therefore, this activity has become a way of life for them. They tend to spend money on products they don't actually need just because they are on sale. This shopping frenzy is what's causing the increase in sales for both classic and online retail.

All the stats and numbers related to sales are encouraging entrepreneurs to start their own retail business, physical or online. The popular trend nowadays is to benefit from both worlds, so a store should have its physical form and its online form. Everyone who wants to make some extra cash should try to do this type of activity and not some get-rich-quick schemes that are promoted online.

Selling products online still has a lot of potential, as the advancement in technology allows you to shop anytime, anywhere. You only need a device with an internet connection, and you can buy your favorite pair of shoes, jeans, or any other type of products.

There are websites specialized in just one niche (selling auto parts, for instance), or there are marketplaces where you can find all the possible products that can be sold online. Retail arbitrage will not get you rich overnight, so it doesn't give you false promises. You can still end up with some really handsome profits if you play your cards right. So let's recap what we already mentioned in this book.

Every online store (or physical store) needs to start with an idea, a very clear one, just like a vision. You already made up your mind and know that you want to sell products online, but you don't know yet the products you want to sell. Finding the ideal product may take a few hours or even a few days, but there are a lot of aspects you will need to consider when choosing the ideal product that you want to sell. This is the perfect time to check some of the most famous marketplaces and discover the most popular products. You will need to check the Amazon and eBay marketplace to find the best products to sell online. However, when you decide which product to sell, you don't have to rely just on the volume of sales because you may end up selling the same product as plenty of other merchants.

To get the most out of selling online, you will need to find the right market niche for you. This means a product that has a high demand but a lower supply. When you find your right market niche, you can dream of dominating this market, as this particular market will not have key players with a big chunk of the market share. The competition is not that fierce, leaving you plenty of room to develop and prosper. As mentioned above, the perfect starting point needs to be Amazon and eBay, but you also need to consider Google. You can find the trending products on this platform, and then you can start your comprehensive market research to see how many products are sold, who the key players are, what market share they have, what prices they have. Gather all information about the products and their sellers in order to take a calculated risk. Bear in mind that the right product will have to respect some important aspects:

1. It doesn't have to be too bulky or too heavy. Try to keep the dimensions and weight as low as possible. You will have to ship the products to your customers. It's more expensive to ship big and overweight products. Plus, imagine how much storage space they will occupy.

2. The price factor is very important. That's why your product should have a value between $25 and $50. This price range should assure you a comfortable profit margin and a high volume of sales to increase the overall profit.

3. You may not know exactly how much the acquisition cost will be, but you need to estimate how much it will cost you to source the product (what will be the price per unit). This is how you can start to calculate your profit margin.

4. The product that you want to sell may be popular, but how fast you can sell it? Can you sell one or more units each day? Are you confident that your product will be a hit?

5. Stay away from seasonal products. You want consistent sales all year round, not just in a few months. If you do want to sell these products, you can do it as an additional secondary inventory.

6. How easily can you find these products? Do you think there are plenty of suppliers and manufacturers that can offer you this product?

7. Try to sell simple products, not the technical ones, as you might need to provide guidelines on how to use them and also technical support. Therefore, you will need to stay away from electronic goods.

8. It goes without saying that you shouldn't go for products like food, as

this kind of products is very perishable. You want something that doesn't have an expiry date, as you don't need extra pressure to sell your products fast.

After you have considered all of these aspects, you can move on to the sourcing part. It's time to find the products you need, but you will have to establish right from the beginning what method will you use. You can go for the following:

- DIY (do-it-yourself) products

- Direct wholesale

- Dropshipping

Personally, I would go for direct wholesale, as this is the best method to source for products. DIY products make you spend a lot of time on handcrafting these products, so you will probably not have enough energy or focus on dealing with promoting your products on the preferred sales channel.

Dropshipping may involve minimum effort from you, but your customers will not know your brand, as you place the order for them through a vendor that will ship the products to your customers. Most of us would agree that wholesalers can provide you the products you need, having the right quantity and quality. It can leave you plenty of time to focus on the other important aspects of your business. So let's say that you go with wholesalers. Although it's highly recommendable to try as many sources as possible, you will need to choose from the available options. You can source for products locally or internationally.

There are some pretty interesting places where you can find really good deals on products that you want to sell. You can check the clearance sales or liquidation centers, where you can find products in bulk at a higher discount than the normal retail price. Discounts can go as high as 70%, so these are great choices when it comes to sourcing for products.

Big retailers have their special designated shelves or corner that are packed with products on clearance sales. Don't be ashamed to check these spots because they can provide you great deals. Liquidation centers are those special places where the clearance sales from chain retailers are centralized in one spot. You will find over there a huge number of products with phenomenal discounts. Also, don't forget about the local wholesalers, as they can have great offers for the products you are looking for.

In order to make sure that you don't miss out on any of these opportunities, you need to keep an eye on social media and your email (you might receive notifications about products having clearance sales or liquidation or special offers). You can even use some apps to make sure that you don't miss any special opportunities.

The Google Chrome browser is compatible with some interesting extensions that can help you find the best offers for products to source. These options all involve going physically to these places and meet the wholesalers who are having these events. You can also source products from behind the screen of your computer as you can find amazing deals online. Some of the great platforms to source for such products are eBay and Craigslist. These are some of the most useful websites a merchant can use. They can easily find some of the best offers online, and they can also find some product ideas if they check eBay. Craigslist may look like a totally unappealing website, but don't let this fool you. The offers you can find here can be extremely attractive because there are products being sold with a massive discount or just given away.

Most merchants disregard this source when it comes to finding a large number of products, but you would be surprised by the products you can find here. eBay is known for its online auctions, and it's a great marketplace to find cheap products online. There are even wholesalers present on this platform who can start an auction for their large inventory. You might find some interesting products in there, and the prices are very low.

All of the sources mentioned above are for finding products locally, within the United States. However, there are plenty of merchants out there who prefer to source for products abroad, especially in China. You will have to deal with shipping costs, customs procedures, and import taxes, but the price of products in China makes all this hassle worthwhile.

The greatest platform you can use for this process is Alibaba, which is the haven of manufacturers and suppliers. This marketplace is the place where companies from all over the world can meet with Chinese manufacturers and suppliers. Alibaba has a set of rules that all the companies present on this platform will have to respect. You can find here suppliers and manufacturers for all kinds of products, including the one you need. All the Chinese companies can communicate in English, and their facilities are inspected by third-party auditors, which will allow them to do business on this platform. Such regulations rule out scammers and fraudsters, so you can mostly find trustworthy companies. Plus, the trade assurance option will be like an extra guarantee that the process of sourcing products will go smoothly, and if it doesn't, you can file a dispute against the company from China. The communication process is extremely important. It allows you to make them understand what the product requirements are, and it can also help you a lot during the negotiation process.

Don't put your trust in the Chinese suppliers or manufacturers. In order to be sure they understood your product requirements, ask them for a sample. Don't ask only one supplier or manufacturer for a sample. Make sure you ask at least five of them so you will have more options to choose from. The price should not be the decisive factor when choosing an offer or a sample. At this phase, you need to make sure that quality is above everything else. If you have to choose between a product that has a lower quality but is within your budget and another one with superior quality but slightly out of your budget, go for the one with superior quality. These Chinese companies are open for negotiations, so you have high chances of getting a price within your budget if you negotiate with them properly.

Now that you have your products, you need to decide where to sell them. What sales channels should you use? There are a few options available, but in order to maximize your sales, you need to sell on multiple channels. You may have your own website that is already optimized, but nothing beats Amazon's traffic. In order for your product to be visible to a higher number of potential buyers, selling on Amazon is a must. Now you can make your life easier on this platform if you choose the right fulfillment option. Fulfillment by Amazon (FBA) is a bundle of services that includes the following:

- Using storage space from Amazon's warehouses

- Shipping the products to the customers at preferential rates

- Outstanding customer support service

- Handling of refunds and returns

- Checking the status of your inventory

- Measuring your performances

- Private brand labeling

These are just a few benefits of using this service, but before you jump in and select this option, you still need to understand the downside of it. You need to choose your products carefully, as you can't risk having slow-selling products. There are storage fees that you need to pay, so you need to keep having an appropriate size for your inventory, plus you need to make sure that your products are selling fast enough.

The cost for the fulfillment service is also something that you will need to consider, alongside the risk of mixing your products with the ones from another merchant. Since there are already many third-party resellers present on this marketplace, if you don't choose the right options, you might get your products commingled with those from other merchants. You can avoid this situation if you choose the labeled products option. You can mark your products correctly with your label so that Amazon will put it in the right spot. Therefore, you will avoid the situation of sending another merchant's products to your customers.

When you choose FBA, your products will be visible to Prime members, which is a community of buyers that have a lot of privileges on this platform, including free shipping. FBA can make your products to be a lot more visible, but this option may be used by plenty of third-party resellers on this platform.

Optimization and advertising can make your product appear on the first page of the results, but this may not be enough in order to convert the views into sales. You will need high-quality images and content, and your price has to be close to other similar or identical products.

Reviews will convince the users to buy your products. Reviews are social proof that the product has high quality and meets the requirements and specifications mentioned in the product description. The service you provide, from confirming their order to delivering the product to the customer (and making sure that the product was delivered), will matter a lot when it comes to reviews.

Not all customers will bother to leave feedback, but if you provide the best support, follow up to check their opinion related to the product, you will definitely get more reviews. The more sales you have, the more reviews you will get, and the better ranking you will have.

It's highly recommended to use Amazon as the primary sales channel if you are selling the right type of products. Additionally, you can also use your very own online store, where your customers will be more aware of your brand and will know exactly where they are buying from.

Having your website properly optimized is a must. Using advertising will also increase your visibility, and if you even integrate e-commerce solutions like Shopify, you will maximize the efficiency of your website. Depending on your choice or the products you sell, you can have your website as the primary sales channel. Other options for selling online can be the eBay platform. This website is more famous for its auctions and has plenty of users worldwide. The only issue with it is that the website doesn't allow you to get in touch with your customers, as eBay protects the contact details of the customers.

You shouldn't use eBay as the primary sales channel, as the customers buying from you will not have a clear idea where they are buying from. This platform can be used just to get additional sales, but you can still make a handsome profit on this platform.

With retail arbitrage, it is highly important to diversify your options and sources. Never rely just on a single source or method. Try to use as many as possible, whether you are sourcing for products or choosing your sales channels. After all, if you do both parts right (sourcing and selling), you will maximize your profit margin and boost your sales as well (this will lead to getting a jaw-dropping profit). So forget about MLM schemes or Ponzi schemes when trying to search for ways to make money online. Try retail arbitrage instead, as this procedure has a huge potential.

Conclusion

Retail arbitrage is one of the most legit ways to make money online, and it is also a method that is gaining more popularity each day. People who want to make extra cash online are already fed up with the false promises made by some websites that claim that they can get you rich in no time. Everyone needs to set the right expectations and start being more realistic than naive. There are plenty of proven ways to make money online, so you have more options to choose from and stay away from different scams and fraudsters. Selling products online is one of the most promising activities you can have. You can start slow, like a hobby, and you might even think of quitting your full-time job to focus on your online business (as it's paying off quite quickly).

Most of the people are consumed by a shopping frenzy. Some of them are even shopping addicts, as they spend money on buying stuff that they don't need — at least for the moment. They buy the products just because it's on sale. Let's face it! Do we really need another pair of shoes if all the other ones are in good condition? There are too many people who are now shopping to impress. This trend has grown way too much, and it's beyond control, as there are so many people buying products on debt. They spend more money than they can actually earn, and this can mean great news for the banks, as they can easily issue more and more credit cards or personal loans. The credit card has slowly become a sort of ID, as most of the adults nowadays use a credit card (most of them have their names on it).

The growing trend of consumerism has caused the sales of products to explode over the past years. More and more merchants are starting their online selling business (or brick and mortar ones) to speculate the shopping fever that has influenced most of us. Retail and online sales are a few of the most dynamic and competitive domains, so in order to always be one step ahead of your competition, you will need to follow the instructions and advice mentioned in this book.

To maximize your profits, you will need to find the best deals out there in order to get a massive number of products to sell. The profit margin is the difference between the retail price (the price you use to sell your products) and the cost per unit (what will be the price per unit for sourcing products). It should cover all of your expenses, from storage to shipping, paying rent, and paying salaries. After all, the volume of sales is one of the most important factors that can influence your overall profits. The success of your business depends on how well you do both parts of retail arbitrage: sourcing and selling. Serious companies have their own procurement departments, so the process of acquiring products or spare prices at minimum prices has huge importance for a business.

This is why most of these companies use all sorts of systems to integrate e-procurement processes.

Of course, the sourcing and procurement process can be different for a company activating in the trading business, and another one that is a manufacturer. Imagine the importance of this department for Amazon Retail (the giant retailer itself). Keep in mind that a majority of products is sold by Amazon itself, so the procurement department really does a great job in finding all these products that are being listed as Amazon products.

Sourcing is a lot more efficient when you purchase huge amounts of products, as it can lead to a very low price per unit. Imagine the leveraging power for Amazon, when the greatest retailer contacts supplier regarding some specific products. These suppliers or manufacturers are willing to lower the price per unit when they need to process a huge order. The size of the order plays a decisive role for the unit price, so as a small merchant trying to grow on the Amazon marketplace, you will need to know that the more you order, the better price per unit you will get. However, sourcing is just the first part of retail arbitrage. The second one is just as important as the first one. If sourcing is decisive for the profit margin, the second one (selling) is more important for the volume of sales, but also it has a role to play in determining the profit margin. You will need to find the best techniques to help you with your sales. Bear in mind that when your product is displayed in the search results list, it's highly important to be listed among the first results, as most users will not even bother to check products listed on the third, fourth or fifth page. Most of them only click on the first two pages.

To increase your visibility and your ranking, you may need to use the best SEO strategies. Try PPC advertising, all to get better rankings. All these techniques can place the product where you want, but in order to sell, you will need high-quality content, pictures, and most importantly, plenty of positive reviews. Nothing can convince potential buyers to order your product like positive reviews, so you will need to make sure that you will get as many as possible. You need to know that if you have the best price per unit in the sourcing process, you can win any price war that your competitors may provoke. It means that you literally have more room to cut down on prices, to a level your competitors will not afford to sustain. Therefore, sourcing done right can help you a lot with increasing the volume of sales. Both of these parts work together perfectly in order to maximize the results of your company.

The ideal situation may be to sell a lot with a very high profit margin. However, at some point, your competitors may lower the price just to get more customers. You can strike back with a better offer because you can afford to lower the prices even lower than your competitor, as the profit margin and volume of sales can allow you this option. If you want to succeed at sourcing and selling online, you will need to go through every chapter of this book and discover how you can maximize both parts of the retail arbitrage process.

References

Art of SEO: mastering search engine optimization (2016). Retrieved from https://www.pdfdrive.com/the-art-of-seo-d27800932.html

Benefits of choosing Shopify for e-commerce store development. (2018, August 08). Retrieved from https://www.orangemantra.com/blog/benefits-choosing-shopify-e-commerce-store-development/

8 benefits of procurement technology tools (2017, July 20). Retrieved from http://spendmatters.com/2017/07/20/8-benefits-procurement-technology-tools/

How to source and manufacture products for your online business (2019, January 16). Retrieved from https://www.bigcommerce.com/blog/source-products-online-business/#undefined

Malik, J. (2019, July 9). Source from Craigslist, sell on Amazon or eBay. Retrieved from https://jordanmalik.com/blog/source-craigslist-sell-amazon-ebay/

The complete guide to sourcing from Alibaba and building an online business (2019, February 1). Retrieved from https://www.bigcommerce.com/blog/alibaba-faqs-security-shipping-taxes/#what-is-alibaba

The top 5 ways we source inventory for Amazon FBA (2019, March 14). Retrieved from https://thesellingfamily.com/our-top-4-ways-to-source-inventory-for-our-amazon-fba-business/

10 best cashback and rewards apps: Are they worth it? Retrieved from https://www.moneyunder30.com/cashback-and-rewards-apps-are-they-worth-it

Wallace, T., Goldwin, C., et al. (2019). The definitive guide to selling on Amazon. BigCommerce, retrieved from https://www.bigcommerce.com/blog/selling-on-amazon/

Ward, S. (2018, December 24). 4 ways to corner your niche market. Retrieved from https://www.thebalancesmb.com/how-to-find-and-master-a-niche-market-2948380

Ward, S. (2019, June 25). How do brick and mortar stores compare with online retail sites? Retrieved from https://www.thebalancesmb.com/compare-brick-and-mortar-stores-vs-online-retail-sites-4571050

What is eBay? (n.d.). Retrieved from https://ecommerce-platforms.com/glossary/what-is-ebay

www.ingramcontent.com/pod-product-compliance
Lightning Source LLC
Chambersburg PA
CBHW071556210326
41597CB00019B/3274